D1228243

THE SYMPHONIES OF MOZART

Wolfg. Amade Mozart

Silhouette by Hieronymus Löschenkohl, Vienna 1785

G. de Saint-Foix

THE SYMPHONIES OF

MOZART

LONDON  MCMXLVII

Dennis Dobson Limited

FIRST PUBLISHED IN GREAT BRITAIN IN 1947 BY

DENNIS DOBSON LIMITED
12 PARK PLACE
ST. JAMES', LONDON SW1

Second Impression 1948

LES SYMPHONIES DE MOZART (MELLOTTÉE, PARIS 1932)
TRANSLATED FROM THE FRENCH
BY LESLIE ORREY

MADE AND PRINTED AT
THE WESSEX PRESS, TAUNTON
SOMERSET, ENGLAND
28/R

CONTENTS

LIST OF ILLUSTRATIONS

INTRODUCTION

To survey the different stages of the 'symphonic' evolution of Mozart is in fact to survey his artistic career almost in its entirety. Between the age of eight and his thirty-second birthday one can easily distinguish at least a dozen periods of 'symphonic' activity, succeeding each other with only two interruptions. And what changes can be observed during the course of these periods! The study of each of these will reveal the degree of seriousness and intensity reached by Mozart in instrumental composition. Also, his contemporaries considered him first and foremost as a master of instrumental music, and were apt to reproach him for treating the human voice as an instrument of the orchestra. In France especially, the first critical appreciations saw Mozart as the composer 'superior on the instrumental side': bear in mind that his symphonies had in fact been performed, his chamber music published, in Paris many years before a single one of his dramatic works had been staged.

The memory of the boy Mozart is preserved by the clavier sonatas played with his father or his sister; the memory of the 'Parisian' Mozart of 1788 is centred on pieces of a very varied nature for chamber (e.g., the Turkish March) or concert hall (the 'Paris' symphony). We had to wait more than twenty years after this date—that is to say, about ten years after Mozart had departed this life—for his first great Parisian stage success, a rather baroque amalgam of the *Magic Flute* entitled *les Mystères d'Isis*, to show what he was capable of in the theatre (1801). By then his sonatas and symphonies had long been admired in France.

In proportion as the performances of Mozart's operas followed each other, leading to the triumphs of the *Théâtre Italien*, towards the middle of the nineteenth century, the opinion of his first hearers underwent some modification, and his instrumental music—together with the general mass of the instrumental music of his epoch—became quite eclipsed by *Don Giovanni* and *Figaro*. From this moment we enter a period when Mozart was known only by his stage works; when, curiously enough, criticism was apt to adopt the idea that the master's instrumental music was mostly a mere transcription of his operas, serious or comic; a given quartet or symphony became as it were merely an instrumental version of some dramatic scene or ensemble. People were so dazzled by Mozart's operatic work that they tried at all costs to incorporate it in his orchestral and chamber music.

Now for us, all this music remains absolutely and uniquely instrumental; in all its immense variety one can hardly recognise any precise reminiscence of a theme previously designed for a vocal or theatrical work. As Mozart's theatre is one, so equally are his great symphonic and instrumental creations, and neither one serves as a model for the other; it would be perhaps even more reasonable to maintain that the spirit of the symphony permeates the great moments of Mozartian opera, and that Mozart's writing remains always more instrumental than vocal—thus confirming the testimony of those first critics who, as we have said, agreed in recognising in Mozart a superiority 'dans la partie instrumentale', and a tendency to treat the voice in instrumental fashion. Perhaps indeed we can attribute to romanticism, at that time too intrusive, the inclination to see in Mozart's instrumental output only an exact reflection of one or other of his theatrical works. But it must also be said that, on the one hand the transcendency of the work of a Beethoven that was gradually being revealed, and on the other hand the tendencies of the romantic school growing daily more audacious, relegated all Mozart's instrumental music, and particularly the symphonies, to the second rank. The latter for all men of taste played in fact an intermediary *rôle*, as it were a gradation between the similar compositions of Joseph Haydn and those—regarded generally as on a very much higher level—of Beethoven. Up to the present, at least to our knowledge, no special work has been devoted to Mozart's symphonies, nor even to the most celebrated of these.

Our keenest wish—though perhaps our ambition has greatly outrun our means—has been to attempt to describe the changing and diverse colours that Mozart's orchestra reflected during the brief life of the master. This orchestra was the constant interpreter of all his dreams; it reveals him to us in the infinite and changeable diversity of his inspiration; it is the permanent witness of all his skill and all the variations of his humour. And it is no exaggeration to maintain that whoever has been able to follow Mozart's orchestral thought, in all its manifestations, will on this account have discerned something of the grand lines of his creative thought.

Then, this examination over, we would like also to try to place Mozart's symphonies historically; that is to say, to show them in relation to those of his contemporaries, and particularly to those of Joseph Haydn; this study will form the subject of a final chapter.

Our warmest desire is that this little work shall in some measure help to reveal something of what we have not hesitated to describe as the universality of Mozart's genius. This is indeed a quite recent concept. For the most part the richness of this universe, in which all the sentiments of the human soul down to the most subtle find expression, remains unsuspected. And it is hardly conceivable that so long a time should have elapsed before an attempt was made to understand that there was anything in Mozart beyond invariable grace and charming elegance.

TRANSLATOR'S NOTE

'Les Symphonies de Mozart' was first published in 1932; since then several important additions to Mozart literature have appeared, notably Einstein's revision of Köchel's Catalogue (1937), and three additional volumes of Wyzewa and Saint-Foix's great work (1936, 1939, 1946), which is now complete. The publishers of this present volume have an English translation of the entire work in preparation. In 'Letters of Mozart and his family' (translated and edited by Emily Anderson. Macmillan, 1938: 3 vols.) will be found details of several of Mozart's contemporaries who have been mentioned in the course of the work. Analyses of five symphonies (K.338, 425, 543, 550, and 551) and the 'Haffner' *Serenade* (K.250) will be found in Tovey's 'Essays in Musical Analysis', Vol. I (Oxford University Press, 1935).

CHAPTER ONE

London (1764-1765) The First Symphonies

Symphony in B flat   Symphony in D
Symphony in E flat

IT NOW SEEMS CLEAR that Mozart's first 'symphonic' model, under whose influence he happened to be directly placed when he was writing his first symphonies, was not his own father but a man of incontestable genius (despite his negligence or indolence) whom he met in London as long ago as 1764. We refer to John Christian Bach, the youngest son of the great John Sebastian who, born in 1735, had settled in England in the latter part of 1762. This master, who almost at once became his friend, had recently spent several years in Milan as organist at the Cathedral; in Italy he had been a pupil of the celebrated Padre Martini, the famous scholar of Bologna, and his letters to his old master are full of deference and respectful admiration. That is to say, Christian Bach was decidedly ranged under the Italian banner, strongly backed by the solid discipline of the Bologna monk; nor could he evade the influence of another man of genius, who headed the great instrumental school of Northern Italy: Giovanni Battista Sammartini.[1] We know that Bach's first symphonies were based on these two models, and by the time of his arrival in London he already had a most enviable reputation founded on the great acclamation accorded these works throughout musical Europe.

[1] Sammartini (c. 1700-1775), born in Milan, where he was organist at numerous churches. His output was vast and included a large number of symphonies. (Tr.)

It was therefore a symphony of clearly Italian character that the boy Mozart first came in contact with in London. John Christian Bach, in England, did not modify his symphonic procedure; he continued to build a veritable overture, in three movements, brilliant and elegant, the first movement revealing clear cut dualism between its ideas, the two themes being in opposition to each other, the one strong and rhythmic, the other slighter and more *cantabile* in style. This movement is generally without a development, and with a single re-entry of the second subject in the tonic. The slow movement frequently attains a noble and expressive beauty, and is followed by a short and rapid finale, which most often takes the form of a Rondo with two contrasting episodes, with the rondo theme *da capo*; the support of the musical edifice is supplied essentially by the two violins, in the Italian fashion, with the wind, horns and oboes or flutes, colouring the ensemble lightly and adequately. This form, easy of comprehension, is marked by a charm both lively and distinguished, and by an expression of sensual femininity that made a particular appeal to Mozart's intimate nature.

We should add that the encounter, in Paris, with a great harpsichordist—or rather, even at this juncture, already fully 'pianist'—Jean Schobert,[2] also had such an influence on the boy that it was to make itself felt in a field far removed from that of the great initiator of French romanticism, that same Jean Schobert! We shall see the extent of this influence when, after having left France, he will be called upon to live in a country where conditions are very different, where taste has nothing in common with that prevailing in the French capital.

In London, under the guidance of John Christian Bach, whose elegant clarity he soon began to imitate, Mozart could not thrust from his mind the memory of what his father called the 'miserable Schobert', and in fact the slow movement of his first symphony is impregnated with a dull and muttering sadness, quite characteristic of the Silesian master (K.16).

[2] Jean Schobert (c. 1720-1767), a prominent figure in the history of the period, though his works are unknown today. He settled in Paris in 1760. (Tr.)

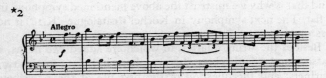

The symphony in question is, we feel convinced, Mozart's first: we are strongly tempted, indeed, to pass over in silence a symphony in B flat (K.17):

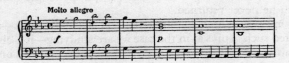

incomplete in its orchestration and containing the four movements of the classical German symphony. With its persistent march rhythm maintained throughout the whole of the first movement, the very short development, its echo effects in the *Andante* and the finale, and its archaic and somewhat forced character, we are led to believe that this symphony in B flat is *perhaps* merely one of Leopold Mozart's compositions—the first minuet in particular has the stiffness and poverty of melodic invention that distinguish the Salzburg *maître-de-chapelle*—that Wolfgang had been made to copy, in the manner of an exercise. The fact is, that right up to his return to Vienna in 1767, all his boyish symphonies without exception will have but three movements and will conform at all points with John Christian Bach's idea of the symphony. Now, here, all the traits proclaim the school of Leopold Mozart, and we can now ask ourselves if we are not faced with one of his recent compositions offered to his son as a school task, an initiation into the symphonic medium. In any case, this symphony in B flat can scarcely rank as number one in Mozart's symphonic works; as we have seen already, it is unfinished; it is, in fact, an essay in an archaic style which the boy quickly outgrew and to which he never returned.

It must be borne in mind that, in a child's work—even granted such genius as in the case we are studying—it is always permissible to ask, not only what was the model for this or that change of style or expression; but even if the entire work whose detail or manner strikes us is indeed the product of his own inspiration, we must never forget that the great, and the most original, masters have copied in the course of their tutelage;[3] copied, yes, and copied perhaps at the order of their teachers. And that is why we mistrust the above mentioned symphony in B flat. The next symphony in Köchel's catalogue (K.18) is no less open to suspicion.

Besides the string quartet, to which are added two horns, a bassoon and a double bass, this symphony in E flat contains two clarinets; and the question of the first use of these clarinets by the young Mozart has been the subject of discussion. These instruments were at that time new to London; two clarinettists had been sent for from there to take part in a performance of a work by John Christian Bach, *Orione*.[4] Now, we have discovered that this particular symphony in E flat— written moreover on the same paper as the exercise of which we have just spoken—is none other than a symphony by the German virtuoso and composer Carl Frederick Abel (1725-1787), published by the latter some years later in his collection Opus VII. Mozart is quite content to score this piece, which provides us with an example of straightforward and honest music without the least spark of genius, or even of originality. But this example is excellent for allowing the boy to learn his trade as a musician; it would certainly have the effect of putting a curb on too original tendencies, which musicians imbued with more modern ideas, as for instance Schobert or Christian Bach, would only have aggravated, without giving the pupil beforehand the indispensable foundations of a sound and solid technique.

[3] The young Mozart's sketch-books are revelatory in this respect.
[4] 1763, at the Kings Theatre. (Tr.)

Abel, whose fame at that time equalled that of his collaborator John Christian Bach, besides being a virtuoso on the viol da gamba was a prolific composer in all the instrumental forms. He played a prominent part in London life and, with the help of Bach, was primarily responsible for the initiation of the English public into all styles of music in some important subscription concerts that were to continue right up to the last years of the eighteenth century. Such, then, as well as his own father, were the boy's first and genuine introductions to the art of the symphony.

But if Abel's skill and science had a beneficial influence on the young Mozart, it is quite evident that the scoring of the E flat symphony aroused no enthusiasm in him. It is obvious that he remained entirely under the spell of the charming and much more original art of J. C. Bach, to which his two first true symphonies can be directly linked.

The one in E flat (K.16) was written in London in December 1764 or January 1765. Even from the time of this first symphony he adopts, and indeed exaggerates, all the devices of J. C. Bach: a clear distinction between the two subjects, the one rhythmic, the other more melodic: repetition of phrases: development consisting of the transposition of the first subject into the dominant followed by expressive modulations after the double bar: and a repeat of the second subject only in the tonic for the recapitulation. The *Andante* in C minor has but a single subject: it is a figure stated by basses and oboes, with triplets in the violins, but this outline is invested with an expressiveness so profound and pathetic that one is immediately reminded of the romantic inspiration of Schobert, whose memory is very much alive in the boy's mind. There are *Andantes* of Mozart dating from this period which, with all due allowances, translate the intimate poetry of his own genius with as much intensity and power as the greatest works of his maturity. As for the finale, it is of exactly the same mould as the symphonic finales of Christian Bach or Abel, deriving directly from the last movements of the Italian overtures of these two masters.

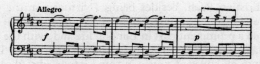

3*

The second of the London symphonies, in D (K.19) was written between January and April 1765. It is modelled, exactly, on the first symphony of Christian Bach's Opus III; but, if it can offer us nothing like the pathetic *Andante* of the former and if its character remains on the whole slighter and more brilliant, we must recognize the enormous progress made by Mozart in the handling of an art whose technique he made his own with an astonishing ease and sureness. When at the end of 1765 he had occasion during his stay in Holland to write a new symphony:

*4

it was still the London model which inspired him: perhaps the presence of a little *coda* at the end of the first movement, perhaps the character of the *Andante*, as of a French '*complainte*',[5] betray a departure from the manner of Bach. But these are of little importance; it is always with the fluency of Bach that we associate the whole of this third symphony of Mozart (K.22).

---

[5] *Complainte*, a folk-song on some tragic or pious subject. (Tr.)

Leopold Mozart

Engraving by Jacob Andreas Fridrich, from Leopold Mozart's
Violin-Schule, published in 1756, the year of Mozart's birth.

CHAPTER TWO

Salzburg
and the arrival in Vienna (1766-1768)

Symphony in F major

Cassation in B flat   Serenade in D

AND NOW WE SEE Mozart back in Germany, apparently taking himself and his work well in hand. He plunges into the study of counterpoint. Contact with the old masters, as well as familiarity with Fux's *Gradus ad Parnassum,* develops and consolidates his knowledge; at the same time there is all around him a new atmosphere, that of his own country, which has a share in making his music fuller, stronger, while at the same time preserving its quiet, penetrating vigour. But despite these factors of musical transformation Mozart remains obstinately attached to practices that his London master had himself never pursued with a like persistency: during the whole of 1767—a year of study and reflection—the characteristic Italianisms of Christian Bach are retained in all his instrumental movements; i.e., neither development nor a return of the principal subject in the tonic key. Once one has penetrated Mozart's mind one can, fairly safely, place this or that undated composition in this or that period of his life, for with him the use of a particular procedure is so consistent as to determine almost a period in his life, after which, like a child, he will abandon it, to return to it only long afterwards or perhaps never. And this correspondence continues throughout the whole course of his life.

Immediately on his return to Salzburg the young Mozart was

eager to show his fellow citizens all his new accomplishments, to demonstrate all the progress he had made during his grand tour.

He has epitomised them in a curious symphony in F major:

*5—K.76.

of which neither the date nor the original manuscript are known to us, but whose style and details indicate clearly that it was written towards the end of 1766 or in the first months of 1767. Already this important composition has four movements, and already it presents the viola parts *divisi*, a characteristic of his Viennese period; the wind parts also (two oboes, two bassoons and two horns) acquire a new importance, especially the bassoons, recalling certain passages in the Abel symphony previously copied by Mozart in London. But in it the composer, with an astonishing tenacity, displays the technique adopted there under the influence of Christian Bach, consisting, as we have already said, in putting the first subject in the dominant, after the repeat bars, and then being content with the return of the second subject only in the principal key. Mozart, in introducing the minuet into the symphony, begins here with a magnificent example: this minuet, welded to the trio, has a breadth and power hitherto unknown; it is derived from his own genius, for the example of such vigorous unisons and such a beautiful finish impels one to question how, by what sudden inspiration, could the youthful composer have attained such a result. And the finale, the principal subject of which evidently derives from a celebrated French dance, the gavotte from Rameau's *Temple de la Gloire*, is also a capital movement, at least equal in importance to the first movement; the form adopted is Sonata Form, but still without the return of the first subject, and it ends with a longish *coda*, similar to that which concludes the first movement of the Hague symphony in B flat (K.22).

During the course of this year, 1767, Mozart was obliged to exercise himself also in the *genres* bordering on the symphony, *genres* much esteemed in Salzburg; he wrote, in response to definite commissions, a *Cassation* (or Suite for orchestra), and a symphonic *Serenade*, which completed his instrumental production. *Cassations* were little symphonies comprising seven or eight movements intended for the embellishment of Court feasts or the family parties of rich burghers, or even as diversions in the solemn meetings of the University; they were occasionally performed in the open air, and displayed a freer, more popular style than symphonies properly so-called, and even than the *Serenades*. The latter contained a fixed number of movements (five), and between them was usually played a little concerto for one solo instrument, or a *Concertante* for several soloists. These pieces were generally played in the evenings, as their name implies. Those scored for wind instruments were played in the open air and were little more than dances; the others, the great symphonic *Serenades*, were intended for one performance only, in exceptional circumstances: great marriages, solemn distributions of prizes at the University, etc. . . . Like the *Cassation*, the *Serenade* opened with a march. In 1767 Mozart, both in the *Cassation* in B flat[6] and the *Serenade* in D— which was published, naturally without the concerto, in separate parts by Breitkopf under the title *Sinfonia*—employs all those devices which we have noticed in his true symphonies, but with a tendency to give a more homely turn to his themes, to lengthen the repeats of his minuets, to adopt numerous episodes in his rondos, under the evident influence of the prevalent customs of Salzburg; also, too, in response to the taste of a man who was gradually to acquire an ascendancy

[6] Saint-Foix gives no Köchel number for this. If it is K.99, both Köchel and Anderson (Mozart's Letters) give the date for this as 1769. Grove gives 1766-1767. (Tr.)

over the boy greater than that of his own father—a man at times careless and erratic, but who carried enshrined in his soul such poetry that he was the personification of all the simple and sincere art of Salzburg, perhaps one might even say of South Germany. This was the younger brother of the illustrious Joseph Haydn, Jean Michael Haydn (1737-1806), Kapellmeister of Mozart's native town since 1762.

On the route between Vienna and Olmütz the young Mozart scribbled yet another symphony (K.43), also in F major:

*6

whose *Andante* turns out to be only a transcription of an air from his Latin Comedy *Apollo et Hyacinthus*. This, moreover, will be the last time he shows himself the devoted disciple of Christian Bach. Later, he will turn again to his London master, but now he is on his way to make contact with the great musical German city; he is going to storm Vienna, there to breathe a new air, in surroundings where Haydn already plays an important *rôle*. It is there that, without yet fully comprehending it, he will experience something of the music of his glorious elder contemporary, and will hear music of masters less illustrious but who, unconsciously, will contribute towards the completion of the structure of the modern Symphony.

CHAPTER THREE

Vienna (1768)

THE YEAR 1768 IS to mark for Wolfgang a time when he will have to put forth a great effort in the triple field of sacred, dramatic and symphonic music, an effort so enormous that one would scarcely believe his frail constitution capable of withstanding it. Quite apart from two Masses, one of which is now lost, his *lieder*, and his Church music, the score of his opera *La Finta Semplice* runs to 558 pages. This score, which despicable intrigues prevented from reaching the stage, was followed by the German operetta *Bastien und Bastienne*, adapted from a French libretto by Favart. Forced to display himself as a composer under these triple aspects a child twelve years old has never, I am sure, performed a like task.

In the branch of instrumental music two symphonies only had been known until very recently: the one written right at the beginning of his stay in Vienna and which was to serve, some months later, as the overture to *La Finta Semplice*, the other dating from 13th December 1768, chock-full of innovations resulting from his stay in Vienna, and which could well be the very first original symphony to spring from Mozart's pen. But a quite recent discovery, by a scholar, M. Fischer, at the monastery of Lambach, has brought to light a symphony of which only the first bars had been known, noted in the supplement to Köchel's catalogue.[7] It had been offered to this

[7] See No. 221 of this supplement (doubtful works); it seems to us quite probable that the symphonies No. 220, 222 and 223, still unknown today, may belong to this Viennese set: they would date from the summer of 1768 and would thus complete a symphonic period more important than one could previously have supposed.

monastery by Leopold Mozart, on 4th January 1769, probably during a stay made by the two travellers while on their return journey to Salzburg.[8]

At a first glance over the score of this unknown symphony one can judge the progress made by the young Wolfgang during the first half of his stay in Vienna. Curiously, while the other two dated symphonies contain the four movements of the classical symphony, this has three only. It opens with an *Allegro maestoso* (G major):

*7

An energetic and powerful theme rumbles in the basses beneath a string *tremolo* and sustained chords on oboes and horns; it concludes with a perfect cadence in the principal key; the second subject is quite short and leads immediately to the first theme again, in D, on the violins, which in fact dominate the movement; it is considerably extended, and allotted to the basses, with the violin *tremolo* persisting; and the first part of the movement ends with an operatic *ritornello* finishing in the dominant. After the double bar this preponderant theme returns even stronger in the bass with a cadence afresh in the dominant. Then, suddenly, there are fierce unisons, on all four stringed instruments, first on C, then B flat, leading to a short passage, expressive and modulating. Finally, the rugged theme reappears once more, first in the violins, then in the basses, concluding with the same operatic *ritornello*.

The *Andante* (in C) is a short *lied* in two parts, stated by the first violins (*con sordini*), and accompanied by basses, *pizzicato*, and horns. The finale, *presto* (3/8), is a Sonata Form movement with repeat bars, double exposition of the initial subject, followed by unisons and rapid *ritornelli*; a curious figure

[8] See *Mozart-Jahrbuch* (Drei-Masken-Verlag, Munich), 1923, pp. 35-69

emerges in the second violins after the double bars, and is followed by new unisons and a recapitulation closely corresponding to the exposition.

Mozart's two other dated symphonies attest the revolution provoked in him by Viennese art. Already the first, (K.45),[9] written a month after the one he had scrawled at Olmütz, is imbued with an entirely new spirit, and henceforward we find a development provided; the *Allegro*:

*8

with no repeat marks, perfectly justified Mozart's choice when, some months later, he turned it into the overture to his *Finta Semplice*, after suppressing the minuet and carrying out various changes indicative of the progress made under the stimulus of the Viennese symphonists. The *Andante*, for strings alone, calls to mind some German comic opera *arioso*, as does the *Andante* of the symphony recently discovered; and the same applies to the pastoral character of the minuet and its *trio*, in which Mozart repeats all the first part. As for the finale, it would figure with advantage among Joseph Haydn's early symphonies; and one remains impressed by its dramatic character.

When, twelve months later, Mozart wrote his other dated symphony (13th December):

*9

[9] Saint-Foix gives no Köchel number for these two. (Tr.)

this dramatic expression will be seen to be still broader and deeper. This symphony (K.48), as much by its style as by its technique, is truly one of Mozart's original creations; with its first *Allegro*, (3/4), full of contrasts and originality, furnished this time with a long development, in which we encounter some pathetic modulations; and which no longer shows any influence of the English symphonies; with its *Andante*, a veritable German *lied*, interrupted by a most unexpected dramatic interlude, a song whose simple and active movement has a very Haydnesque heartiness; with its grand Viennese minuet, of so singular a beauty; with its finale ecstatic with vitality, ending in a novel *pianissimo*, we find ourselves confronted by a work that surely entitles us to herald the great symphonist—who is to achieve greatness before having written a single sacred or dramatic masterpiece. But here, besides a purely instrumental ideal such as masters like Joseph Haydn, Vanhall and others, representing the new classical symphony, inspired in him—and including perhaps the last representative of pre-classical art, the aged, lively and charming Wagenseil— we must recognize that another element has appeared to enliven his music. We are indebted to the theatre and the drama of Gluck and Hiller for those sudden interruptions in the musical weft, for those unexpected and wild effects that so brusquely startle the listener. Wolfgang must have had experience of the theatre for his *Finta Semplice*, or for his one-act opera *Bastien und Bastienne*; and whether it was the drama of Gluck, or French or German comic opera, he was thereafter no longer inspired by the masters of purely instrumental music; or, rather, since the latter themselves succumbed to the deep and passionate sentiments expressed by the first 'romantics', by the trouble and anguish permeating all music—how was it possible for the impressionability of Mozart to resist such impulses?

CHAPTER FOUR

Italy (1770-1771)

The first two visits

ON HIS ARRIVAL IN Italy Mozart's first impression of the 'symphonic' art of that country was principally derived from hearing operatic overtures, performed at concerts as well as in the theatre. Such overtures did not emanate from 'symphonists' properly so called, who were moreover rare in Italy. The opera composers belonged either to the old school, writing for the most part *opera seria* according to the old Hasse-Jommelli formula, or they had surrendered to the new taste for *opera buffa*, which at that time was accustomed to have a shorter and more compact overture, written often in one movement (Paesiello, Piccini, Sacchini). This, then, was the sort of thing Mozart encountered on his arrival on Italian soil.

The symphony here, then, is most often an *overture* pure and simple, and nothing need hinder its being played at the opera before the rise of the curtain; the Italians, moreover, delighted to hear it again in the concert hall, where it is fully suited to open or close an 'Academy' programme; often the three movements will be linked together and played without a break. The short slow movement offers but a brief interruption to the brilliant and varied play of the first *Allegro* and the finale; the themes will often be repeated in the manner of the theatre, where they pass from one character to another; the subjects will be clearly differentiated; they will be more numerous than in the Viennese or German symphony, so that the contrasts can be brought out with more clearness. These subjects are apt to be shorter, more

25

precise, and will often give the idea of a juxtaposition rather than an elaboration; they will often be provided with long *ritornelli*, flowing and brilliant, such as may be found on every page of the operatic aria (or vocal sonata); and if in the course of one of these Italian symphonies we are struck by syllabic repetitions in the themes or by the shakes which round off the theatrical *ritornelli*, this is but what we should expect from opera. Wind instruments (horns, trumpets and oboes or flutes) are very busy; they are scarcely independent, but bolster up and sometimes overburden the ensemble. As for the pattern of the movement, the Italian masters adopted impartially the system of development, with a return of the first subject in the principal key; or the absence of development—that is to say, with the main theme repeated in the dominant: in this case the second subject only reappears in the original key. But there is also a simpler system still, in which the movement leads right on to the end without any recapitulation, with the subjects in juxtaposition and, by their character, in opposition to each other. This latter system became established more frequently after about 1770; it is not unusual, on the contrary, to find in the finales of these symphonies, also very short and rapid, a return to the initial idea.

Mozart adapted himself readily to this new conception, but he was not to remain faithful to it for long, because within a year of his arrival in Italy he discovered that despite the preponderant taste for the theatre, that country also possessed a few rare spirits for whom instrumental music surpassed all other music.

Whereas the great majority of the composers of *opera seria* and *opera buffa* practised the system we have endeavoured to describe above, we know for certain that Mozart, soon after his arrival in Italy, had the providential opportunity to get to know, first, the work of the youngest of these instrumental masters and, a few days later, to meet personally the oldest. At Mantua, in fact, as early as January 1770, Mozart had to perform, or probably to accompany, a trio of Boccherini at one of his concerts; shortly after, in Milan, he was to prove his worth before the venerable Jean Baptiste Sammartini, soon afterwards to become his friend. We must say at once that the lesson of high and pure poetry instilled in him by these men was not fully comprehended until a year or two later. At the time of his first contact with Italian art these masters still played no part in his music, while the rest, the musicians of *opera seria* and *buffa*, are clearly in evidence in the first symphonies that Mozart composed immediately he set foot on Italian soil.

It would be as well, first of all, to point out that the period of Mozart's stay in Italy, a period so important from the point of view of his artistic growth, falls into three sections. The first extends from the beginning of 1770 to the spring of 1771; the second from the summer of 1771 to the winter of the same year; and the third from the autumn of 1772 to the spring of the following year. During the course of these three great epochs of his life we shall have to notice numerous and profound modifications in the conception he has formed of the symphony; now the purely Italian influence will be modified by contact with his own country, thrice revisited; now it will be softened still more when, returning from Southern Italy, he again comes to Milan and its Viennese influences. And on his return to this town for the last time he will bring from his own country a considerable amount of symphonic 'baggage' which he will have to combine with new acquisitions, the fruit of his latest Italian period.

In the first two symphonies (K.97 and 95):

*10

Allegro

*11

Allegro

27

which might be called overtures, to be written on arriving in
Italy Mozart, still faithful to Viennese custom, retains the
minuet before the finale; but his movements are already worked
out on the Italian model. He uses alternately the new fashion,
with a recapitulation in the principal key, and the old, wherein
the first subject is repeated in the dominant; the rapidity
with which the subjects follow each other, and the almost
complete absence of true developments betoken in a striking
manner his conversion to his new models; if, in the two
symphonies we can still recognize traces of works written by
the boyish Mozart in Vienna, in 1768, there is no question of
these when he came to write his third symphonic work in Rome:

*12—K.81.

and to complete his fourth at Bologna (K.84, 1770):

*13

Multiplicity and brilliancy of subjects, absence of minuets,
constant repetition of phrases, a much reduced and generally
much more homophonic instrumentation—such are the char-
acteristics of his third and fourth symphonies or Italian overtures; this does not mean that the ingenuity of certain details
or the grace of the slow movements do not reveal in charming
fashion the free evolution of Mozart's genius, adapting itself to
the Italian ideal.

Whereas during the first part of his Italian stay Mozart, busy with his opera *Mitridate*,[10] seems to have been thoroughly absorbed in the theatre, it is very noticeable that by the end of this first year in Italy his instrumental art assumes a form infinitely more refined. In a symphony in G major (K.74):

*14

undated, but probably the last to be written before his return to Salzburg (in the spring of 1771), the usual framework of the Italian overture remains the same, with the *Andante* always linked to the first movement; but the care devoted to detail, the delicate inspiration shown in the *Andante*, which one recognizes as a mingling of Sammartini and J. C. Bach, the ravishing originality of the final rondo, with its two violins only, and the intermediate minor section which they underline with their *pizzicati*, all indicate a profound change in his symphonic manner—or rather a return to the predominance of his instrumental ideal. And to what can we ascribe the change? Perhaps to frequent performances in the *salons* of Count Firmian, a Salzburger, it should be noted, then Governor of Milan; or else to the fine and eloquent treasures strewn among the *Sinfonie per Camera* of Sammartini, just beginning to exert their influence on one who was already no longer a child. Or was it perhaps due to the symphonic compositions of John Christian Bach which, written in Milan, had the freedom of that city, and were being played at the same time as those of old Sammartini?

The fact is that from the spring of 1771—remember that the stay in Bologna during the summer of 1770 had brought Mozart another encounter, with Padre Martini, whom no man in Europe equalled in musical science—Mozart's symphonic work acquired a new relief and independence. We shall see

[10] *Mitridate* (K.87), *opera seria*, produced 26th Dec. 1770 Milan. (Tr.)

his Italianism mingling with the atmosphere of his birthplace, to which, already filled with the ecstasy of Italy, he returned in March 1771.

It is precisely from this moment that, amongst varied influences, Italian or German, the first symptoms of what is to become in the course of time the real symphonic art of Mozart make their appearance in striking fashion. It is highly probable that he wrote, either at Salzburg or Milan, about a dozen symphonies during 1771, namely, K. 73, 75, 98, 110 (July), 112 (November, in Milan), supplement 216, the overture to *Ascanio in Alba*, supplied with a finale for performance as a symphony, and finally, numbers 214, 215, 217 and 218 of Köchel's supplement.[11]

*15—K.73.

*16—K.75.

*17—K.98.

*18—K.110.

[11] These last symphonies figuring in Breitkopf's Thematic Catalogue have not been rediscovered.

*19—K.112.

*20—K. Suppl. 216.

*21 *Ascanio in Alba*, K.111.

These symphonies are, in general, much more instrumental in style than the first Italian ones; one feels most clearly that Mozart does not set out to build his symphonies simply on the pattern then in vogue, but that in writing a symphony he is embarking on a new quest, casting the most deliciously varied inventions in the conventional mould. Sometimes the melodies of his *Andantes* will be stamped with a personal character of gravity or of tender playfulness, or they will be extended to give free rein to lyricism of the purest kind; sometimes he will use German dances or French gavottes in his finales, and he gives some of his minuets a character so original and so unexpected that one cannot distinguish between what springs from his own adolescent genius and that which could have been inspired by the recent creations of Joseph Haydn. It seems certain that some of the symphonies by this master, who from now on begins to exert a visibly growing influence, must surely have been known and admired by the young man. From all these points of view the study of the symphonies composed by Mozart

31

either at Salzburg in the spring, or in Milan during the summer and autumn of 1771, acquires a particular interest and attraction for us: from this moment, in fact, the child is no longer a child, he becomes a creator, he acquires a power capable of assimilating the most diverse tendencies; his style is sometimes Italian, sometimes Austrian or Salzburgian, but even now we can fully recognize the future instrumental style of Mozart.

We can without difficulty observe traces of a new spirit in these different symphonies. Whether the recapitulations are exact or abridged or whether the developments are content to be simple transitions, there are momentary passages of attempts at counterpoint; one feels a growing firmness in the rhythmic design, and something like the need for unity between the different movements; everything becomes freer, more individual, and this individuality not only resists diverse and contradictory tendencies, but asserts itself more and more clearly by an assimilation, a brilliant appropriation, of these. As we shall point out in the course of this study, Mozart's Symphonies are *handled* as Italian, but *felt* as German.

CHAPTER FIVE

The Symphonist (1772)

RETURNING TO SALZBURG IN the last days of 1771 the young man felt tempted to offer his new employer—the Archbishop of Salzburg, Sigismond de Schrattenbach, had just died, and his successor was imbued with very modern ideas—some varied proofs of his musical talent; moreover, Mozart's sixteenth year sees him devoted entirely to symphonic preoccupations and grappling with the gravest æsthetic problems.

1772 is a period of extraordinary maturing for him, so that, from the particular point of view that concerns us here, we can say that Mozart then attained in the domain of symphonic music a grandeur, surpassed later, but never achieved by means of such giant strides. Alas! that we must confess that since Mozart's time, no one has had direct testimony of this; the eight symphonies he wrote between December 1771 and August 1772 were published for the first time in the great Breitkopf edition, but it has not occurred to anybody to perform one,[12] and we are led to believe that only the scores are in existence.

Here are the openings of the first two:

*22—K. 114   Salzburg, 30th December, 1771

[12] The Paris Symphony Orchestra has recently (before 1932—Tr.) performed the symphony in E flat, K.132.

*23—K. 124   Salzburg, 21st February, 1772

The musical world would be overwhelmed with a combination of admiration and astonishment if these eight symphonies could be revealed today; in them Mozart's instrumental ideal is realized not merely powerfully, but completely. This ideal, it is true, continues faithful to the Italian taste; but the widening of this taste is such as to raise the question whether the young Salzburger has not here given to the *genre* of the Italian overture a beauty and power never before achieved, or even foreseen. With a marvellous clarity, suppleness and solidarity this German has probed the innermost secrets of the sense and proportions of the Latin *chef-d'œuvre*; he saw how to adapt it, without upsetting its dimensions, to the mould of what was to become the German Symphony, with all its resources of orchestration, its richness, its profound inner unity. It is true that when he wrote his great symphony in D, about July 1772, he had a model before him; this was Joseph Haydn, the Haydn of 1770 or 1771, a man in the prime of his youthful force and activity, giving primarily the impression of vigour, of heroic spontaneity. Mozart drank in his music with avidity, but his own temperament added to it an Italian element of poetic beauty, sometimes artless and quiet, sometimes burning and fiery, which allied itself with the often rustic force of his glorious senior. The evidence of this symphony in D is so arresting that the most frigid commentator could not help but be gripped with astonishment. But this one is exceptional; on Mozart's return to Salzburg his mind is still full of Italy, and he sets about producing two short symphonies in C and G:
*24—K.128.

*25—K.129.

suppressing the minuet in order to return fully to his trans-
montane ideals. We know, moreover, that during 1772 it
was the custom at Salzburg for the symphonies of J. C. Bach
and Sammartini to be performed at the concerts or 'Academies'
which took place from five to eleven o'clock.[18]

It was especially these two masters that he glorified and
transfigured right up to the moment when, curiously enough,
he came to understand the symphonic art of Joseph Haydn.
One might have thought that his efforts would at first have
been directed towards the latter's brother, Michael Haydn, the
Salzburger, whose genius seemed to be more nearly allied to
his own; but we must expect all manner of surprises in dealing
with a mind so versatile and receptive as Mozart's. The fact is
that about the end of May 1772 he presents us, after the short
symphonies in three movements just mentioned, with what we
may boldly call the first of his great symphonies. This is the one
in F major (K.130):

*26

It opens with a rhythm destined later to depict the clownish
fury of Monostatos, in *The Magic Flute*. We wish we could
reveal to the reader something of the future horizons that this
work heralds, and even achieves; we are here faced with a new
world that no pen could describe. A veil torn apart by the

[18] Hanslick—*Geschichte des Concertwesens in Wien.*

35

unconscious thrust of genius has dropped from the young
composer's eyes. The barriers have broken down under the
stress of widening and deepening; the whole of the symphony is
steeped in the spirit of Italy, but this time it is Mozart alone
who displays and bestows the acquired riches; *bizarrerie* and
boldness in the minuets, tender delicacy in the *Andantes*,
gaiety or whirlwind force in the finales, strength and power in
the design. Something of all this we can see, too, in a symphony
in E flat (K.132):

*27

which he perfected in the spring of 1772; and particularly in
the last, the astonishingly imaginative and poetic one in A:

*28—K.134.

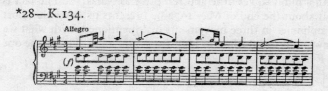

of August of that memorable year. All the musical qualities of
his preceding symphonies—the thematic elaboration, the
enhanced expressiveness of the recapitulations, the richness due
to the use of violas and wind—all are to be found here, with,
in addition, the innovation of *Codas* concluding the movements
and separated by double bar lines.

Although Haydn's influence manifests itself but transitorily,
we can however say that all Mozart's symphonic production in
1772 bears the general mark of a vigour and youthful animation
rather similar to those qualities that permeate Haydn's sym-

phonies of 1770. The latter in 1772[14] had undergone an acute crisis of 'romanticism' whose repercussion Mozart would assuredly have felt had he been acquainted with the works Haydn wrote in 1772; moreover, he himself, at the time of his last visit to Italy, was on the point of being racked by that same fever that, besides the qualities noted here, was to produce those pathetic outbursts, the heavy restlessness, that distinguish the '*Sturm und Drang*' movement which, at about this time, was to seize the old world. Heroism, youthful force of Joseph Haydn in his symphonic production of 1770-1771: heroism, youthful force of Wolfgang Mozart in 1772, his sixteenth year. In this very year he caught up with the older composer—his senior by twenty-four years. But if Joseph Haydn's inspiration made itself fully felt only when Mozart wrote his symphony in D (K.133):

*29

nevertheless he had already appropriated all Haydn's solid vigour and had added to it, under the impulsion of the Italian masters and his own genius, that gift of pure and sovereign beauty which, in truth, belongs to him alone.

. . . .

As we have said already, it was at the time of his third and last visit to Italy that the young Mozart evinced signs of this romantic 'crisis', whose causes are perforce unknown. It may have been due to his age, to some physiological condition he was faced with; if we do not know of any striking event of this sort in his life, perhaps we may attempt an explanation

[14] See in this connection a study by T. de Wyzewa, drawing attention to this crisis and its 'symphonic' importance, in *Revue des Deux-Mondes* (15th May 1909).

of an æsthetic order, which moreover would be sufficient to account for a profound change in outlook.

It should be noted that this state of mind seized him after finishing his *Lucio Silla*,[15] and that this drama is not wanting in several passionate scenes, set by Mozart with a truly poignant depth of feeling such as the rest of the work seemed scarcely capable of inspiring: he is there content to give the instrumentation a new luxuriousness, but his heart is not in it; whereas in the graveyard scene where Giunia, accompanied by a chorus of attendants, evokes the shade of her father there is an emotion, a tragic grandeur, which immediately recalls Gluck. One might ask whether Mozart at some time or other while in Italy had not had occasion to hear one or other of the operas of the German master; or perhaps there had been some old tragic Italian capable of kindling such a flame in his heart . . . The fact remains that accents can be found there which had not previously been heard in his music. It should be noted that this vein of romanticism in Mozart is displayed especially in his chamber music; in particular, the string quartets and sonatas for violin and piano[16] written in Milan during this last visit to Italy, with their variety, their high relief, and the depths of the sentiments expressed, remain the truly incomparable witness of his first emotional excitement.

In the purely symphonic field the examples are limited to the overture to *Lucio Silla* and to another symphony in C major

*30—K.96.

whose sombre, dramatic and bold character led Wyzewa to conjecture that it might at first have been intended for the over-

---

[15] Produced Milan, 26th December 1772. (Tr.)

[16] These have been recently re-published under the title *Sonates Romantiques*.

ture to *Lucio Silla*. Without counting also the overture to *Sogno di Scipione*, to which Mozart added a brilliant finale to turn it into a symphony independent of the *pièce d'occasion* to which it served as an introduction:

*31—K.126.

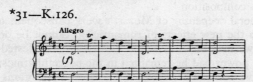

The distinguishing mark of the first two is primarily a care for *nuance*, shown by a veritable profusion of *p*, *fp*, *pp*, *ff*, etc., an unaccustomed procedure with Mozart, serving as a hallmark of this period of his life; next, an inspired grandeur which embraces the movement as a whole and takes cognizance of the tiniest detail. Wyzewa in particular emphasizes the resemblance between the development section of the *Andante*, in the over-ture to *Lucio Silla*, and the style of the big scene in the first act, whose especial character of nobility and romanticism we have already commented on; but one is above all struck by the use of the wind instruments whose blare, punctuating the brilliant and rapid string passages, gives to the whole of this brilliant overture a proud and heroic quality. And here once more, beneath the wholly Italian nature of the work, we sense the German master who has just completed the 1772 symphonies, so varied and solid. The same is true to some extent of that mysterious symphony in C (K.96), of whose exact date of com-position and intended purpose we are ignorant; everything here breathes a sort of dramatic solemnity that evidently suggests some theatrical adventure in a sombre key. It is all compact, concise; and the more concentrated the style, the more direct and eloquent does the expression become; the *Andante* especi-ally seems constrained by dint of the effort to be expressive, and one gets the impression that Mozart is checking the free development of his melodic genius in following the bareness of some model unknown to us. As the symphony contains a long and beautiful minuet before the finale we can scarcely suppose that we have here a work intended for the theatre, but the proximity of the drama *Lucio Silla* may be presumed to be not without influence on the original conception of this very mysterious composition.[17]

The general deepening of Mozart's work consequent on his yielding to the new effects of romanticism cannot be denied; his work, we may be sure, would never have manifested such expressive power had he remained in the peaceful atmosphere of his native town. The worth of his latest acquisitions from Italy is beyond price. If, returning to Salzburg in the early spring of 1773, we see him reverting readily to the taste of his own country, there are several compositions which still show how profoundly the latest Italian 'shock' has disturbed him. And these works are precisely those symphonies—or, rather, veritable overtures—constructed of three movements leading into each other, after the fashion of the Italian overture such as Mozart had been hearing while journeying south of the Alps.

Four had been written there, possibly in response to the request of some Milanese patron. The orchestra is that of his *Lucio Silla*; and a single glance over the score of the most remarkable of these four overtures will give the reader an idea of the power of this orchestra and the height of expressive concentration to which it is brought, after the attempts noted above (K.184, in E flat):

*32

The violence of the first movement followed by the infinite despair of the *Andante* (in the minor), and the ardent and joyous rhythms of the finale mark this symphony as something quite apart; romantic exaltation here reaches its climax, and

[17] K.96—Number 157 of our new classification.

the succeeding overtures have nothing, or hardly anything comparable to offer. Moreover, a quite recent discovery seems to present curious confirmation of our suppositions in regard to this dramatic prelude.

We know that Mozart, during 1773, had to compose the music for a philosophical drama, *Thamos, King of Egypt*, libretto by an Austrian official, Baron Gebler. Mozart's contribution was limited to writing some entr'actes and choruses that the librettist had hoped to entrust to Gluck. The 1773 version is almost unknown to us for Mozart, taking up the work again in 1779, partly remodelled it, and then added a melodrama; it is in this remodelled form that a German scholar has just discovered, at Frankfurt, a score of *Thamos*, but under the title: *Entr'actes et chœurs de Lanassa, par M. le Maître de Chapelle Mozart*. The music of *Thamos* is adapted to another libretto, an extract from a French piece by A. M. Lemierre, *La Veuve de Malabar*, which had had a great success during the eighteenth century, and was played in German as *Lanassa*. The author of the article, Herr Otto Bacher,[18] explains that the first notion of this transformation came to a friend of Mozart, Johann Böhm, director of a travelling theatrical troupe, whom he had known well at Salzburg when the company played there in 1779-1780, and with whom Mozart lodged while passing through Frankfurt in 1790: it seems certain that he was present at a performance of *Lanassa*, and that he had agreed to this transformation of his *Thamos* as long ago as 1785. Böhm is also the author of the German version of *La Finta Giardiniera*. The two pieces, it appears, maintained their place in the repertory at Frankfurt and in the Rhineland for a considerable length of time. All this leads up to the question of the overture to *Lanassa* for, in contrast to the score of *Thamos*, which never had one, *Lanassa* did have an overture, which the author of the article does not seem to know. Now, judging from the first bars cited by him, we are faced with none other than our symphony-overture in E flat, which it is particularly curious and interesting

18 *Ein Mozartfund. Zeitsch. f. Musikwiss.* January 1926, pp. 226 *et seq.*

to meet again here! We can well conceive that Mozart had
never lost sight of it, and chose it to serve as a prelude to the
romantic drama of *Lanassa*—the German version of that *Veuve
de Malabar* who, unable to endure the loss of her husband, ends
by throwing herself into the flames of an Indian funeral pyre!
Remember, too, that *Thamos* can trace its origin back to 1773,
like the overture in question; who then, if not Mozart, could
have found it after so long a time, considering that it had never
been published? However that may be, the choice, probably
Mozart's, is significant, and the overture is in every way better
adapted to the dishevelled romanticism of the French play,
which is infinitely more alive than the philosophical, or
rather Masonic, lucubrations of Baron Gebler.

The other overtures in the same series, in D, C and B flat:

*33—K.181.

*34—K.162.

*35—K.182.

do not offer the interest of the first (Ex.33); they do, however,
give an impression of fullness and orchestral vigour which is

very striking. Although the form is that of the Italian overture, the working out of this form yields an impression of vigour and solidity productive of complete musical satisfaction. The usage adopted by Mozart for the slow movement at this time (*andantino grazioso*) agrees very well with the style of these three overtures; and the theme of this *andantino* has the exquisite fragrance of an oboe melody full of lyrical feeling. Moreover, the first movement of this overture in D (K.181) promises us tragedy of the same order as the preceding overture; but it is quickly sacrificed, to make way for a working out in which imitations play a larger part than one would expect from the opening. The finale, a sort of quick-step, is not without inducing regret for the rich variety and inexhaustible invention of the Rondos of Mozart's last Italian period.

CHAPTER SIX

Vienna and the return to German influences (1773-1774)

'THE MUSICAL *milieu* OF Salzburg had sufficed to turn Mozart aside from the Italianism of the preceding years; but it had not the means to substitute a new artistic pattern of a cut to satisfy a genius grown so mature and profound as Mozart's. And under these conditions one can understand the immense import at this juncture for the young Mozart of the visit to what Burney rightly calls "the capital of the musical world", to the city of Vienna, where he was to find an answer to the questions that were troubling him, and a clear indication of the route he was to follow'.[19] Although the Mozarts had stayed in Vienna during the summer season of 1773, that is, in the holiday period, they would have had the opportunity of hearing much instrumental music—the best in the world for stimulating in Wolfgang a renewal of his symphonic art, which is to make itself felt, not during the few months stay in Vienna but, in due course, after his return to Salzburg.

The English traveller Burney notes the presence in Vienna during the autumn of 1772—i.e., a little before the arrival of Mozart—of so many masters of music that we can easily imagine how important this visit would be to the young and enthusiastic musician. 'It will suffice', says Burney 'only to mention the names of Hasse, Gluck, Gassmann, Wagenseil, Salieri, Hoffmann, Haydn, Ditters, Vanhall and Huber, who have all greatly distinguished themselves as composers; the symphonies and quartets of the five last mentioned composers

[19] T. de Wyzewa and G. de Saint-Foix, *W. A. Mozart*, vol. ii, page 43.

are perhaps among the first full pieces and compositions, for violins, that have ever been produced'.[20] In contact with these works Mozart set about acquiring a complete professional mastery which remained with him all his life. Counterpoint is reawakened in his work with a new vigour, for Haydn had just written a magnificent set of quartets, several of which ended in fugues; and the same applies to those, then quite recent, of the scholar Gassmann, who had been a pupil of the venerable Padre Martini. So we must not be surprised to see the youth, scarcely arrived in Vienna, dashing off a set of six string quartets, two of which likewise end with fugues! But this is not all. The first work he wrote in Vienna was a grand *Serenade*, intended for the marriage of a Salzburg notability, Herr von Andretter; and in this work we can see Haydn's style reigning supreme. Mozart has perhaps never written a work in which he so closely followed the teaching of his illustrious elder. We must allow that he could not better have chosen his model from among the remarkable set of composers then in vogue in Vienna, and from now on the prodigy of 1762 and 1768 takes up his place among them. 'We may say that from the summer of 1773 until his arrival in Mannheim, towards the end of 1777, Mozart, in short, remains a true composer of the Viennese school.'[21]

It is impossible, then, to over-emphasize the importance to Mozart of the lessons learnt in Vienna. It is clearly in Vienna that he became acquainted with Haydn's symphonies of 1772 which, with or without such characteristic titles as *La Passione* or *The Farewell* or the *Symphonie Funebre* all reflect the intense crisis of romanticism Haydn went through in that year; to these must be added several symphonies of Vanhall, an artist of similar temperament though unequal inspiration. On the other hand, such masters as Gassmann and Ditters, smitten by *opera buffa*, are in process of creating a Viennese instrumental style, which, light and lively, is to have the sharpest reaction on Mozart.

[20] Burney, *The Present State of Music in France and Germany*, vol. i, page 364. (Tr.)

[21] Op. cit., vol. ii, p. 45.

After Vienna, then, we shall see his developments lengthening, his *Codas* becoming weighty *résumés* of his first movements and finales, the finales themselves rivalling the first movements in importance and assuming the Sonata Form; in a word, a more elaborate workmanship, a language more clearly symphonic, a more pronounced breadth given to all his instrumental compositions. As almost always happens with Mozart, this serious style is not going to last very long, for 'la galanterie' is about to overrun the whole of music. But we can say that Mozart in his symphonies of 1773-1774 has reached the end of a period, and that after it he will not do better, but different things.

Afterwards there will be Mannheim, and Paris; his orchestral masses will be more powerful, the horizon will be wider; but for all that, something of great intimacy and charm will have disappeared; the subtle perfume of Vienna, combined with the Italian flavour, will have vanished. Mozart's incomparable youth, as evidenced in his 1773-1774 symphonies (though, alas, too rarely experienced) will be over.

Did Mozart, on reaching Vienna, intend to complete the set of Italian overtures written on his return from Milan? This is not unlikely, for a *Sinfonia* in G major (K.199):

*36

with the *Andantino grazioso* typical of this set, fits absolutely into the framework of these overtures. But at the same time this curious instrumental piece, brilliant and Italian in style at first, shows such peculiarly Viennese qualities that we have at times the impression of hearing echoes of the orchestra of Johann Strauss. Rhythms of Viennese dances follow each other in all three movements and—a significant point—the finale opens with a sort of *fugato* that soon takes on a waltz rhythm;

46

decidedly we are in Vienna. The Austrian masters of the eighteenth century saw nothing incongruous in this mixture of styles; examples could be cited from Michael Haydn, and probably from many more we do not know! What is one to make of the finale of the first of Mozart's great quartets (that in G), dedicated to Haydn? What of this fugue, interspersed with such lively and gay refrains?

Thus, in the great symphonies composed by Mozart in the latter part of 1773 and during the spring of the following year, we shall come across echoes of that humour whose extreme subtlety is to be found in the almost contemporary *La Finta Giardiniera*. These symphonies, four in number, certainly count among Mozart's grandest; and it is a matter for regret that, following these, he should have abandoned that high ideal of great music which filled him at the time, in order to turn towards 'la galanterie'—ravishing, no doubt, but in which one feels a secret shrinking from all that broadens and deepens music.

What is the impulse behind the birth of these four grand symphonies? One can see in them a sort of 'sublimation' of the compositions of the two Haydns—for, since his return to Salzburg Mozart felt himself more and more attracted by the work of his *confrère* and friend Michael Haydn, whom of course he very quickly surpassed in originality and intensity of expression. Mozart was indebted to Michael Haydn for that ideal poetic beauty of certain of the *Andantes*, a kind of reverie which often attained the summit of his artistic creation. For Michael Haydn, despite his native indolence, had the soul of a poet which revealed itself, not only in some admirable sacred music, but also in his symphonies and chamber music, by melodies of an infinite tenderness, and dances of a quality and harmonifation intimately 'Mozartian'. Haydn's career, unfolding itself side by side with Mozart, in the same town and the same procession, gave the latter the benefits of a quasi-providential teaching and friendship.

But quite certainly we shall come across nothing in his symphonic production that is the equivalent of these four symphonies of Mozart. Never, simply from the harmonic point of view, could he have written the opening bars of the symphony in A (K.201), in particular—a symphony which may be considered one of Mozart's most characteristic instrumental masterpieces, one in which he is already completely himself:

*37

and as for the symphony in G minor (K.183):

*38

it is already such a promise of the famous masterpiece of 1788 that we can look for explanation only to the young man's genius. The fire he kindled there burnt only in his own soul. Granted, the full working out of such thoughts is not yet perfect, and cannot be; in the *Andante* for example, there is a second subject that has no affinity with the first, and whose banality offends us, and in the first movement we are conscious of some voids. But that startling and breathless opening, followed by one of the most arresting themes of the *Don Giovanni* overture, that wild *Coda* and the sinister drum roll to end it, whence do all these arise, if not from the very depths of Mozart's soul?

And if, now, we examine the first of these four symphonies, that in C (K.200):

*39

with its heroic grace, and its minuet, worthy of Mozart's grandest creations, we shall have the satisfaction of studying a work that foreshadows its successors while losing nothing from their proximity: perhaps, on the whole, the slow movements of these symphonies do not quite reach the level of the other movements, but the essential fact is that there is nothing that really impairs the works. It must however be admitted that the last, in D (K.202):

*40

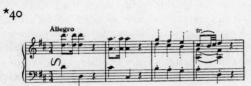

despite the cleverness of its scoring, does not quite belong to the same class. It dates from 5th May 1774, and Mozart's thoughts and feelings have already changed.[22] The emphasis now is on entertainment, and the 'galante' symphony has no other object. With the exception of one or two overtures he will write only *divertissements* and *serenades*, until the moment when he finds himself, in Mannheim and Paris, in fresh contact with a great symphonic school.

In this symphony in D the themes follow each other but are never unified, although speaking generally their fellows in the preceding symphonies achieve that profound unity which Mozart, in his great creative periods, always strove to attain. Although we must regret this changed outlook, it is a sign of the times: the invasion of the 'galante' style is also obvious, and quite as noticeable, in the work of Joseph Haydn. His symphonies entitled 'The Schoolmaster', 'Imperial', and 'Fire', in which we can detect no traces of the great works of his romantic inspiration of 1772, do, in fact, date from 1774. The Esterház master, more lively and nervous than ever, had sacrificed his old ideals entirely for 'la galanterie'. And in his symphony in

[22] Op. cit., vol. ii, p. 141.

D Mozart follows the same path; we can easily recognise, in the short and delightful *Andantino*, some of the significant chromaticisms of the astonishing symphony in A (K.201); but the unexpected and rather vulgar buffoonery of the finale, despite an originality which approaches the grotesque fury of Osmin in *Il Seraglio*, cannot make up for all we admired with such good cause in the preceding finales.

Such are the thrilling symphonies with which the 'great creative period' of Mozart's life closes; their scope is greater than any of the works we have noticed so far. The lessons learnt in Vienna, the daily intercourse with a master of the calibre of Michael Haydn, the deeper and deeper understanding of the works of the latter's elder brother, and even of those of the other Viennese symphonists—all this was consummated in these four works which, at each new reading, provoke our astonishment and admiration; to these elements we must add the extraordinary maturing of his genius. We very much doubt if any youth, on completing his eighteenth year, has ever shown an equal effort or produced comparable beauty.

CHAPTER SEVEN

La Galanterie (1775)

AS WE HAVE ALREADY said, Mozart, for four successive years, entirely abandoned the great classical ideal and yielded to a lighter, more worldly art, more in keeping with the 'galante' taste which had at that time possessed the world of music. It is now a question of amusement rather than emotion. His style on the whole remains what it was, but the inspiration is slenderer, its import less. The slow movements alone—and perhaps, curiously enough, more often than in the past—will give rise to some admirably poetic reveries infinitely surpassing the charming but unvarying gaiety of the other movements. If Mozart's present 'galante' period does not permit a symphony, we cannot pass over in silence the various orchestral *serenades*— bulky ensembles clearly allied to the symphonic *genre*—which are spread over the period between 1774 and 1778.

Every summer, for wedding and anniversary feasts at the houses of the rich burghers of Salzburg, Mozart had to write one or two of these *serenades*, consisting of five usually very long and brilliant movements, besides a violin concerto which was always interpolated. The prevailing mood of these *serenades* is decidedly the 'concertante' style; the principal performers are given the opportunity for the display of a certain degree of virtuosity which, however, is kept within reasonable bounds, and as a result never runs the risk of destroying the purely musical interest of the work. But it is none the less true that these *serenades*, being occasional pieces, are more superficial than the symphony proper, and thus closely correspond to the 'galante' ideal; so it is quite natural to find Mozart, between 1773 and 1776, occupied in midsummer in dazzling his fellow-citizens with vast symphonic *serenades*, full at the same time of that Austro-Hungarian good-humour (*Gemütlichkeit*) and of solemnity—festive music interrupted by incomparable minuets, or by melodies imprinted, or rather impregnated, with tenderness and supernatural grace. And in these *serenades* there is such a wealth of felicitous scoring, of dialogues between the *concertante* instruments, such a variety of sentiments (more marked perhaps than in the symphonies), that one is justly astonished to see so much learning bestowed on works that, after all, were intended only for the occasion of some anniversary or festival.

Speaking generally, the new attitude is revealed in these *serenades* by very distinct subjects, by short and rapid imitations, by exactitude of recapitulation and by a curtailment of the *Codas*, lately so beautiful, which now become (except in certain of the *Andantes*) no more than unpretentious little *stretti*. It was customary for the *serenade* to open with a march in which, in general, the first part never reappeared in the recapitulation; with Mozart the initial rhythm of the march was often recalled in the first *Allegro*, thus giving a noticeable unity to the whole. But on the whole there was no elaboration, no really extended working out; the variety and freshness of the themes replaced the cohesion we so admired in the symphonies of preceding periods. Here, in music full of fire and brilliance, Mozart seems to concentrate his attention on the *Andantes*, whose beautiful melodies and poetic expression compensate for the too rudimentary nature of the other movements.

In the year 1775 in particular this taste for *divertimenti* and *serenades* is apparent on almost every page Mozart wrote. The opera he had to compose in the spring of this year was itself a *serenade pastorale*, *Il Re Pastore*, on a famous libretto by Metastasio. Its overture, in one movement, is to serve as the prototype of the great operatic overtures of his maturity; but being written in 1775 it, very curiously, could not avoid being transformed into a *serenade!* Mozart is content to transfer the first air of the opera to the oboe, and to add a grand finale which is one of the most lively and witty Rondos he has ever produced:

*41—K.102.

The theme is a sort of French contre-danse, with all the minor intermediary sections intentionally omitted, as too contrary to the prevailing 'galante' ideals. But the animation of this finale and the ingenious return to its initial theme invest this work with a quite peculiar charm and give it an importance that totally escaped Mozart's first biographers, who wrongly attributed it to a period before 1770. In order that the scheme of the *serenade* might be complete Mozart, on August 20th 1775, wrote a superb march in C major, opening with a bold unison *à la française* which, obviously, was intended for the opening of this curious pastoral *divertimento* (K.214):

*42

It should be added here that the presence of a French contredanse gives rise to the supposition that Mozart must have had at hand some collections of French dances at about this time, which were not without their effect on him. In fact, he used several of them in the finales of his contemporary violin concertos; and this practice could have been suggested to him not only by these collections but by the violinists of the French school, who were even then addicted to the concerto 'on well-known airs'.

We have no doubt that Mozart was acquainted with the works of several of the most remarkable representatives of the French Violin School; neither Gaviniès, nor, notably, Le Duc nor Guénin[28] were unknown. Amongst the concertos of these last two artists there are some striking, even disconcerting, 'Mozartisms', which prove the *rôle* played by the great French school in Mozart's conception of the violin concerto. We shall have moreover in a short time to consider the importance of this *rôle* in the domain of the symphony proper.

[28] P. Gaviniès, 1726-1800. Marie A. Guénin, 1744-1819. Simon Le Duc, 1748-1777. 'Grove' gives some details of their lives. (Tr.)

CHAPTER EIGHT

The Haffner Music (July 1776)

The twentieth year.

*43

THIS *serenade* (K.250), composed by Mozart in the middle of his twentieth year, that is to say, in the full flower of his musical inspiration—for this year, 1776, sees the full blossoming of his rarest gifts of music and poetry—this *serenade* marks for us the climax, not to say the apotheosis, of the period we have designated as 'galante'. It is the successor of the *serenades* of 1773, 1774 and 1775, but with what a difference! Its exceptional length is perhaps due to the solemnity of Elisabeth Haffner's wedding (she was the daughter of the Burgomaster of Salzburg); but it is certain that on this particular day the young master was bent on making a great impression and spreading out before his fellow-citizens all the richness his genius was able to produce. It is really, in every sense of the word, a musical *feast*, in which Mozart gives free rein to his fancy, creating almost new forms; where, too, rhythms to be used later in his *Don Giovanni* make their appearance before our delighted eyes . . . So that the late burgomaster's *salon* becomes as it were the antechamber of the philandering nobleman bent on some new and ephemeral conquest.

Within the limits of 'galante' music, since all idea of depth and severity is banished from the musical scene, since all is effectiveness and brilliance, it seems scarcely possible to go further; not that, on the other hand, emotions at once attractive and tender are not occasionally revealed (in the long *Andante*, a concession to the Salzburgers' taste for prolixity), or a development of the most highly lyrical kind (in the other *Andante*, in the Concerto). All this—the abnormal length of the movements, their variety, their brilliance, the elaboration of detail entrusted to a big orchestra—all this almost compels the adoption of the new 'galante' ideal; but on reflection, one feels all the same, both in the first movement and in the *Allegro assai*, the great hunting song with which the *serenade* concludes, how different is such a work from, for example, one of the symphonies written by Mozart a year or two earlier. Despite all the attractiveness—which is great—of this musical feast, this copious banquet, one cannot conceal the weakness of certain movements, the inordinate longueur of the Rondo, in G, and also of the finale. And one begins to regret the high artistic endeavour which endears the former symphonies to us, even though these may have nothing in them to equal the two amazing minuets of the *Haffner serenade* in which Mozart, with an unmatched maturity, anticipates the ballroom scene in *Don Giovanni*.

In the period we are studying, the young master, as we have shown, gives free rein to the virtuosity of his soloists, and writes concertos for most of the instruments of the orchestra calculated to show off their qualities to the best advantage—but never allowing mere brilliance to cramp the inspiration of the moment. This virtuosity, too, is ranged over a wide field; he does not content himself with opposing one performer to the orchestral mass, but divides the orchestra itself into several groups and makes them 'concert' among themselves. On the other hand, he is fond of using an 'echo' device, probably taking the idea from some model unknown to us; that is to say, he will write a phrase more or less long, given out by a quarter o f the performers, the remainder finishing it, or repeating it as an echo. But the repetition may only be partial, or even confined to quite a few bars, or the end of the phrase, or even its very last note: but always with particular care that this repetition is, like an echo, an exact textual reproduction of the preceding. This echo device, moreover, was practised by eighteenth century masters such as Haydn and John Christian Bach; the former specified that the *Echo* ought to be played in *separate rooms*, but this pleasantry appertained rather, we think, to chamber music. In his symphonies for two orchestras, on the other hand, John Christian Bach, in the spacious rooms of the London Pantheon, used two orchestral masses responding to each other. Mozart in his *Serenata Notturna* (K.239—N.C.242):

*44

—which is itself not strictly an echo—uses two small orchestras, one formed of two principal violins, viola and double bass, the other of two violins, a second viola, 'cello and drums. The idea here is, evidently, a dialogue exchanged between two small orchestras placed some distance from each other, as for example at each end of a room; and one can easily see that if the echo procedure is not consistent, it is employed very wittily. The other composition of the same *genre* is, on the contrary, a veritable 'echo,' entitled *Notturno* (K.286—N.C.283):

*45

written for four orchestras, each of two violins, two horns and bass. As with the first, we do not know the occasion for which it was composed. The echo device is used with remarkable understanding of its effects; thus, the fine *Andante* with which the work opens has a first subject of four bars repeated in its entirety by the 'first echo', after which the other orchestras take up fragments only, getting shorter and shorter.

Sometimes, to give the effect of a more distant echo, the reply is reproduced only after a period of silence; sometimes, again, in a *stretto* the repetitions appear, first at a bar's interval, then a beat apart, then two beats, in canon; and thus we see the final perfection bestowed by Mozart on a phenomenon of nature known to us all.

In the sequence of his symphonies which we shall see growing in nobility and beauty all these *serenades* and *divertimenti* sound a note of 'galante' variety illustrating the taste of his compatriots, and belonging to a *genre* at the same time solemn, homely, and even frankly popular, peculiar to Austria and South Germany. In them we see the old orchestral Suites, *Cassations* or *Serenades*, infinitely rejuvenated and revived by the genius of Mozart, and no study of his symphonic compositions with any pretensions either can or should neglect them.

CHAPTER NINE

Mannheim and Paris (1777-1778)

Quartet (or Sinfonia) Concertante
'Paris' Symphony (K.297)
Overture in B flat

THE GRAND TOUR UNDERTAKEN by Mozart in company with
his mother in September 1777, which was to be prolonged
until the early part of 1779, marks an epoch of capital importance in his short life. From this time he ceased in some
measure to be the Salzburg musician, to become the universal
master. It is not the practical result of the journey that should
be considered, but rather the considerable enrichment, the
broadening, if we may say so, of his art. The young man tasted
independence, wider horizons opened before him, grave events
ripened him prematurely. The young and agreeable musician
of Salzburg was to become, in a few months, the great, the
immortal, Mozart.

One feels clearly, moreover, that he had need of a change of
air, that the atmosphere of his native town was inadequate, from
the sole point of view of instrumental music, to slake his thirst
for novelty. So we behold him in Germany's 'symphonic' town
par excellence, that old Palatinate city wherein instrumental
music had acquired a more weighty importance than anywhere
else. At Mannheim, in fact, each member of the orchestra
seemed to fulfil an official mission, so seriously did he take his
functions; the wind, notably, attained a perfection which made
an immediate and vivid impression on Mozart. But—a curious
and almost inexplicable fact—he did not write a symphony! It
is only much later, in Paris, that he turns to account the

essentially 'Mannheimist' resources of the orchestra. In the meantime he writes only for piano, violin, voice or flute, and his music betrays strong French influences.

It is indeed very surprising that a musician such as Cannabich, whose friend and guest he was, and who kept him in constant touch with every detail of his own compositions, never encouraged him to confide to the admirable orchestra anything more substantial than his praises. It is true that, if musical interpretation there was superior, it cannot be said that Mannheim, at the particular time that Mozart was there, could boast of anyone to rival Michael Haydn, the Salzburg master, in musical worth or personal genius. For Mozart the only person who really counted in this School was old Ignace Holzbauer, another Viennese, whose *Günther von Schwarzburg* founded German opera and re-echoed in the very depths of his soul. This art, strongly tinged with Italianism, was very much more likely to please him than that of a Vogler or a Schweitzer, or even, dare one say it? a Gluck. And as for the symphonists past and present of Mannheim, he gives scarcely any details as to the real value of their works. But he remains struck in particular by the admirable instrumental ensemble, by the timbres and their effects; especially we can say that the clarinet was revealed to Mozart during his stay in Mannheim, and that he was then granted a prophetic glimpse of the marvellous resources it was to offer him in the future.

It is now no longer to be a question of charming Salzburg *divertimenti*; his music henceforward will work towards two main ends: solidity of writing and, especially, a sort of delicately graded precision in the expression of feeling. Until then he had been content to interpret these feelings in general rather than in detail. The new elements absorbed during Mozart's five months at Mannheim are to serve as excellent preparation; he is still in close touch with the prevailing French taste, for the Palatinate was, in fact, a French colony. Charles Theodore, the Elector and reigning sovereign, was a man of entirely French culture; his architects more or less always took their lead from Versailles; all the great 'Mannheim' symphonies of Toeschi and Cannabich, without exception, were sold, published and played in Paris, so much so that Mozart on arriving in the French capital found himself hearing the Mannheim repertoire all over again at the *Concert Spirituel*. At the outset of his journey he had made contact with 'some quite charming pieces' of the Alsatian Edelmann; then in Paris he renewed acquaintance with Schobert's sonatas and got to know those of Hullmandel. The French influence was therefore at work before his arrival in that country; and before actually arriving in Paris he even wrote some *ariettas* to French words.

The programmes of the great Paris orchestra during the early spring of 1778 were composed mainly of the Symphonies of Gossec, whom Mozart had the opportunity of meeting, and of the Abbé Sterkel, whom he reproached for playing too quickly; but these programmes also included Mannheim symphonies, by Toeschi and Cannabich, with in addition numerous *concertantes* designed to group the most diverse virtuosi together and show off their talents to the best advantage.

This latter is a *genre* that we can almost say was born in Paris, about 1770; public demand was for 'solo' instruments in the symphonies, and the growing tastes for virtuosity especially favoured all soloists. Thus, the first proposition made to Mozart, the day after his arrival in Paris, concerned Mannheim's four most famous wind virtuosi, who had come to Paris at the same time as Mozart. The suggestion was that he should write a 'symphonie concertante pour la flûte de Wendling, le hautbois de Ramm, le cor de Punto et le basson de Ritter'.[24] But, we must add, he changed his mind and substituted for the flute a clarinet, the instrument he was so captivated by at Mannheim.

*46—K. Suppl. 9.

[24] This work was replaced by a *symphonie concertante* by Cambini (1746-1823), played by the same quartet (Concert Spirituel, 12th and 19th April 1778).

This, which, like the choruses he had written for Holzbauer's *Miserere*, was prevented from performance by some rather shady intrigues, is a monumental work showing no evidence of the haste with which Mozart confessed he wrote it. It enormously overshadows all the *sinfonie concertante* of the age and even, by its working out, former ones by Mozart himself, and never again will he give us such an example of the art of Mannheim. The spacious designs of this great work, one of the longest he wrote, the marvellous understanding of the resources of the wind instruments, stamp it as a quite unique work, a landmark in the history of both the Symphony and the Concerto. It is a direct consequence of his Mannheim visit, and in it we can see the beginnings of the grand manner of so many of his masterpieces for wind instruments. It is noteworthy that the three movements of this symphony or quartet *concertante* are all in the same key; their length, with Mozart, indicates importance, according to the popular taste at Mannheim, and shows him presenting himself to Paris with a sort of *Concerto grosso*, rejuvenated and brought up to date. There is still no decisive French influence; the work remains German in both conception and working out. If Mozart wrote it in Paris it seems to have been conceived in Mannheim, and at a time when he had as yet had no direct contact with any specifically French art; there is, in the serenity of the *Adagio*, a kind of religious sentiment akin to Beethoven, and it is no exaggeration to claim this as one of the greatest moments in all Mozart. The way the ten variations of the final *Andantino* follow each other, with the intercalated *tuttis* which never play the theme, but only the refrain, is itself an inspiration; but the penultimate one, leading to an *adagio* recitative which prepares the way for the final acceleration, once more carries us towards Beethoven, while the unexpectedness of the calm before the end removes us from, or rather lifts us above, the 'thème populaire' that is the main theme of this remarkable finale. After all, perhaps the work as a whole was deemed too different from what the subscribers to the *Concert Spirituel* were accustomed to hear, and no doubt this is the sole reason why this vast *Concerto grosso* with which Mozart hoped to make his Paris *début* was never heard.

A compensation for this first failure was not long in coming. In fact the performance, in June, of his symphony in D, called the 'Paris' symphony (K.297):

*47

concerning which Mozart sent his father some details, seems to have been a great success. However, in order probably the more completely to satisfy French tastes, he entirely remodelled the *Andante* (in G), replacing it by a new movement, in our opinion more facile and less banal than the first. This second version has been preserved, and was even published in Sieber's edition.[25]

It must be said at once that at first glance this symphony marks a striking progress from the point of view of scoring; the Mannheim influence is undeniable. In this work Mozart, solely to please us, adopts the methods of the later 'Mannheimists', in particular those of his friend Cannabich. This is a question of the precise attack by the whole orchestra, what was known then as 'le premier coup d'archet', a phrase which has aroused much sarcasm; of the constant repetition of themes; of the absence of repeat marks, and of an essentially brilliant veneer to the whole work; it seems to us that real French symphonic music had still not reacted on him at the time when he favoured us with this 'Paris' symphony. For who was most frequently performed at the *Concert Spirituel* during his visit? Gossec, unquestionably, whom he met, but who seems to have influenced him only during the latter part of his stay in Paris;

[25] *Bib. du Conservatoire Paris, Recueil No.* 32 (Symphonies) 'Du repertoire du Concert Spirituel: chez le Sr Sieber, musicien, rue St-Honoré entre celles des Vielles-Etuves (sic) et celles d'Orléans, chez 'Apothicaire, No. 92.' This was the first edition.

the symphonies of the Abbé Sterkel were also frequently played, as we have remarked above, also those of Cannabich and Toeschi—without counting the numerous *concertanti* of which the public remained very fond, offering as they did such opportunities to virtuosi of renown.

The conception and composition of the 'Paris' symphony was clearly influenced by the joy he felt in having at his disposal an admirable body of wind players, in being able worthily to employ each one, drawing from them the effects he so revelled in while at Mannheim. These effects were not used by him until his arrival in Paris, to which the leading players from Mannheim had moved at about the same time. The importance of this orchestra and its resources, which Mozart himself has enumerated,[26] led him to write for a stronger and more compact group than that of Salzburg, moreover a group of players who were often also renowned composers. The symphonic result achieved by Mozart in this, his first composition 'for grand orchestra', remains, in fact, quite superficial. The admirable unity we have striven so often to emphasize, especially in the symphonies of 1772-73, does not strike us here; there is not that inward relationship between the different subjects, nor the exquisite originality of invention and working out; they follow each other without amalgamating, and it must certainly be conceded that they are somewhat ordinary. Mozart is so sensitive to every influence that he goes to the extent of impoverishing his own natural inventiveness in order to adopt the imposing but quite empty framework that distinguishes the greater number of the Mannheim symphonies; when it was a question of showing off instrumentalists of the first order he created a work infinitely greater and more original; his symphony or quartet *concertante* described above seems to us much more important than the 'Paris' symphony. Only the finale of the latter, opening, *piano*, with the two violins announcing a *fugato*, greatly heightens the whole of the symphony; and this anticipa-

[26] In a letter to his father, 4th November 1777. '10 or 11 firsts, the same number of seconds, 4 violas, 2 oboes, 2 flutes, 2 clarinets, 2 horns, 4 'cellos, 4 bassoons, 4 double basses, trumpets and drums.'

64

Michael Haydn
Engraving by J. F. Schörter

tion of the *fugato* is not wholly deceptive, for the second subject is ranged in a series of imitations; the repeated antiphonal effects between wind and strings certainly make for variety and, also, the passage following the second subject contains a few bars in which we recognise joyfully that abrupt change of key so frequent in Mozart's rapid finales, a sudden veer of the Mozartian fancy which gives to these few disturbing moments a psychological value perhaps superior to all the rest of the work.

The best proof that the 'Paris' symphony decidedly impressed the patrons of the *Concert Spirituel* is that a 'Nouvelle symphonie de la composition del Signor Amadeo Mozart' figures in the programme for 8th September, 1778.[27] This had been lost, with the quartet *concertante*. Some years ago, M. Julien Tiersot discovered in the archives of the Société des Concerts an *Overture*, in B flat, for grand orchestra, published in parts under the imprint of the Conservatoire.[28] We for our own part have no doubt, after examining the score, that we have here what we are justified in calling Mozart's third French symphonic 'monument'.

It would be difficult, from the purely musical point of view, to detect any correspondence between it and the preceding symphony. Apart from the fact that it is scored for the same orchestra,[29] the language, the style, the inspiration, all are different and, despite the inevitable kinship with Mannheim which, moreover, we have shown to be so agreeable to French taste, we can say with certainty that here Mozart really has appropriated something of contemporary French art. If we were now to seek to enumerate the sources to which he was indebted we should have before us a large number of comic opera overtures, Grétry's in particular, which are very likely to have served as models, especially for the *Andante Pastorale* which opens the work and serves as an introduction to the *Allegro con spirito*.

[27] *Journal de Paris*, 1778, p. 987.

[28] *Overture à grand Orchestre par Mozart*. Prix: 9 fr.—à Paris—à l'Imprimerie du Conservatoire, faubourg poissonnière, No. 152. Publishers No. 18.

[29] 2 violins (several parts), viola, 'cello and double bass, 2 flutes, 2 clarinets, 2 horns, 2 oboes, 2 bassoons, 2 trumpets and drums.

However, the resemblance is only of the most general nature and could quite easily have been evoked by any French Sicilienne. In the symphonic works of Gossec, heard by Mozart at each of the *Concerts Spirituels*, there are some 'points de départ' infinitely nearer to this B flat Overture. Not that such overtures in one movement, to our knowledge at least, can be found in the purely instrumental work of Gossec (though this would moreover not be impossible), nor that this work can offer examples of counterpoint of such power; but it would hardly be difficult to find, in some of the 'Pastorales', a similar inspiration. Without venturing outside the French master's Opus 5 one can find the very opening of the initial theme of the *Allegro con spirito* of the overture in B flat.[30]

Was Mozart's aim in writing this work to reduce more and more the extent of a symphony, or to compose a simple *Overture* in the manner of the composers of operas or comic operas? We would be tempted to believe it, if we had not long ago established that the first symphonic work he wrote on his return to Salzburg was none other than a similar overture in one movement, packed with French reminiscences, whose dramatic import suggested, wrongly, that we had here the overture to some unknown theatrical piece. The real truth seems to be that Mozart had for nearly a year adopted the framework of the *symphonic overture*, under the direct influence of impressions received in Paris. More, one may add that the clearly symphonic character of the powerful *Allegro* of the B flat overture has nothing in common with the overture to the ballet *Les Petits riens*—very light and barely tinged with 'turquerie'— which does approach more nearly those of the masters of French comic opera.[31]

The extreme diversity of Mozart's Parisian impressions is apparent in technical procedures that, one feels certain, he would never have used if his memorable sojourn in Paris had not taken place. Alike in his piano, chamber and orchestral music, there are such novelties, a spirit so removed from that

[30] *Symphonie, op.*5, No 1.
[31] See Hermann Abert, *W. A. Mozart*, vol. 1, pp. 733 *et seq.*

of Salzburg, something so pompous, such a feeling of effort, so studied and not without a certain sense of strain, that one is almost disconcerted. And such are the feelings one experiences in the presence of this astonishing overture in B flat. We have here a veritable upheaval in the work and convictions of the young Mozart; the piano sonatas in A minor, those for piano and violin in E minor, the *sinfonia concertante* for the Mannheim soloists—all these, one after another, preceding this overture, give place to a quite chaotic phase in the rapid flowing of the 'Mozartian' flood. It can be said of most of these works, as of the present overture, that we have here a great mind exposed to all manner of external attractions; each of these works taken by itself shows us, often with considerable force, a Mozart in the act of discovering some entirely new idea, models for which, it is gratifying to note, can be found in French music; taken as a whole, it is difficult to believe that these works belong to the same creative period. And moreover, in studying attentively a work such as this B flat overture we cannot, despite its power and real beauty, help being struck by something working rather in a void, something which, as in several works of this period, at times gives, too, the impression of skimpiness. All this, moreover, will need nearly another year for it to be thoroughly assimilated; only in the works dating from 1779-80 shall we see the full fruition of Mozart's grand tour.

On the whole, his symphonic production during his stay in Paris show him evolving by clearly marked stages towards the French style;[32] still very 'Mannheimist' in the quartet *concertante*, he conforms more to French taste in the 'Paris' symphony, though still remaining faithful to the Mannheim school; the overture in B flat shows him already a slave to French manners and customs, but with a persistent dramatic idea such as is apparent in the symphonies and overtures of a Gossec or a Gluck.

[32] Parisian symphonies 'del signor Amadeo Mozart' continue to figure in the programmes of the *Concert Spirituel*: March 18th, March 28th, May 23rd, June 3rd, 1779 (advertisements in the *Journal de Paris*).

We feel we ought to give here a few brief details of this overture in B flat, which is not available in a modern edition; the themes are worthy of notice, if only to give an idea of the quality of Mozart's inspiration during the latter part of his stay in Paris. (K. Suppl. 8).

The overture opens, as we have said, with an *Andante Pastorale:*

*48

34 bars long, the theme allotted to the first oboe *solo*, accompanied by sustained chords on the strings. We need not here stress its typically French character, reminding us at once of Grétry. The first violin replies to this in a passage linking it to the *Allegro Spiritoso:*

*49

We have already compared this with a symphony by Gossec (Op.5, No.1), of which the following are the opening bars:

*50

This first subject, repeated, leads to a theme of martial character:

*51

briefly rounded off by a concluding *ritornello* in the dominant. Then begins a true development on the first subject, which is repeated at the commencement in the original key. A new cadence in the dominant ensues, and a solo for the bassoons:

*52

The bassoons are soon joined by the flute alone, and then comes a little *fugato* leading to the recapitulation. This begins strictly, but is modified after the following fashion: the *ritornello* of the first part is suppressed, instead, a development of a passage which has figured in this *ritornello* here serves to separate the two expositions of this first subject. This second appearance of the first subject corresponds fairly closely with the second exposition in the first part; but this time a passage is momentarily suppressed to make room for a return of the beautiful bassoon theme, this time played by flute and oboe in the tonic. After that, a *ritornello* on the first violin (in triplets) leads to the suppressed passage, adorned with a brilliant final *ritornello*. The scoring is distinguished by contrapuntal force, solidity and marvellous brilliance.

CHAPTER TEN

The Return to Germany (1779-1780)

Symphony in G (K.318)
Symphony in B flat (K. 319)
Serenade in D (K.320)
Concertante for Violin and Viola (K.364)
Symphony in C (K.338)

SINCE MOZART DURING THE years 1775 to 1777, both before his great Mannheim tour and while he was in France, wrote no symphonies properly so called, one may well feel some astonishment on finding him, once more returned to Salzburg, applying rapidly the techniques that have just revealed to him a school very different from that of his native town. Whether this unexpected recrudescence of his symphonic productivity was the result of an order from the Archbishop, or whether it was simply one more indication of his interest in orchestration we cannot say; but we may well believe that, back in this narrow and backward town that he disliked, he could not resist the temptation to give his compatriots some idea of both Parisian tastes and his own improved abilities. From all the memories seething in his brain he chooses first of all something heroic, pathetic, something at the same time very frank and clean in expression, with new and very varied nuances. This something was the outcome of a very real intercourse with the French masters and, although he remains absolutely silent on the subject, probably also with the Opéra or the Opéra-Comique. All the projects he had cherished in this regard in France came to nothing, and these frustrations must undoubtedly have helped to embitter him and indispose him towards the French: Mozart owed us, in fact, a lyric tragedy, *Alexandre et*

70

Roxane, both poet and libretto of which remained unknown to him. But we can console ourselves with the fact that these preparatory studies of Mozart and his father's counsel on the subject of French taste led up to Wolfgang's first dramatic masterpiece, the lyric tragedy *Idomeneo*, whose origins can be traced back to that same Lemierre,[33] the author of *La Veuve de Malabar* which we have previously mentioned.

There is already a touch of *Idomeneo* in the first symphony, in G (K.318), written by Mozart two months after returning to Salzburg:

*53

the theatrical flavour might even suggest an overture, though otherwise there is no justification for such an opinion. The work, a curious one, full of innovations, written in a single movement (there is a slow movement in the middle, followed by an abridged reprise of the first part, as a *Coda*), shows to what extent Mozart had remained impressed by the *opera seria* overtures he had heard in Paris; its explanation is much simpler now that the B flat overture is known to us. On the eve of quitting Paris, Mozart, probably influenced by Gossec or other masters of French opera, writes a symphonic overture in one movement; the moment he finds himself back in the calm of Salzburg we have another work of precisely similar character, just as compact and dramatic, and equally with no precise object in view. Note too that the scoring of the two works is the same, except for the clarinets, missing at Salzburg; but the Parisian work is the stronger contrapuntally, and the whole is in general much more elaborate and developed; the symphony in G, though barer, is not less strong, and unexpected modulations are not lacking; what is more, the middle *Andante* has a character so 'Mozart-

[33] Antoine-Marin Lemierre (1720-1793).

ian' that we feel ourselves on the brink of his maturity. The symphony in G is one of the most convincing proofs of the profound change which has come about in Mozart during his long tour; there is nothing in it of the old Salzburg style, and if he had continued to write in this style one would have been almost justified in saying that Gluck or Gossec had definitely replaced Michael or Joseph Haydn in his heart! The particular spirit and style of this overture are going to make way for other tendencies, until the moment when the Abbé Varesco, adapting the French work of the curious Lemierre to the taste of Salzburg or Munich, evokes the same inspiration, the same brass writing, sometimes the same dissonances. It is needless to add that in all this we have the technique of the Mannheim school used with increasing purpose: powerful *crescendos*, a freer interchange of musical ideas between *soli* and *tutti*, masterly use of the wind, etc.

Some months later, at the beginning of July 1779, Mozart in the symphony in B flat (K.319):

*54

draws for us a delightful picture of a beautiful summer's day; we could almost describe it as his 'pastoral' symphony! It is full of gusto, joy, dancing, not unmixed with a certain sensual ecstasy (in the first movement), expressed by numerous and insistent chromaticisms. This first *Allegro* (3/4) has the captivating undulation of a Viennese waltz; it has no repeat bars, nor could it have, since from the opening to the final *Coda* the dance movement persists without pause. The symphony originally had but three movements; the minuet was added later, in Vienna, accentuating still more the general character of the work. There is, it has even been suggested,[34] a certain resem-

---

[34] Abert, *op. cit.*, vol. i, p. 806, note 2.

blance to Schubert, whose name springs involuntarily to mind But where has Mozart had the opportunity of breathing these rare Viennese perfumes? We seem to hear popular tunes of the Austrian capital in the finale—a joyous *mêlée*, after the lyrical repose offered us in the *Andante*, very skilfully conceived in the taste of the times. Here is certainly a work imbued with the Viennese spirit, abounding in delicious rhythmic and harmonic details which, indeed, have no point in common with the highly dramatic quality of the preceding symphony in G. In the latter there is no difficulty in recognising the dramatic influence, as it were a premonition of *Idomeneo*, but we think it would be much more troublesome to discover in contemporary Viennese masters, the Vanhalls and Dittersdorfs, any work analogous to this B flat symphony. It is, taken as a whole, a mirror of the pure genius of Mozart.

This Viennese spirit, compounded of delicate playfulness and artless sensuality, continues to be apparent in a series of works by Mozart, and is to find an interpreter of similar calibre in certain works by the young Schubert; it is, too, a spirit pervading many a *cassation* or *serenade*, of which Mozart typifies the highest expression. However, since accomplishing his grand tour some foreign elements have intruded, and it is found only rarely in its former purity; we must wait until the last year of Mozart's life when, transfigured, purified by celestial appeasement, it will attain its uttermost beauty.

We do not know the motive behind the appearance of a grand *serenade* (K.320):

*55

still in the customary key of D, dated August 1779: it is as it were the pendant to the Haffner music of 1776, but enriched by all that Mozart had gained since that time. Seeing the introductory prelude suddenly reappearing towards the middle of the first movement we cannot but recall the experiment in the preceding symphony in G, of interrupting a grand *Allegro* by a slow movement; but here the originality is greater since the function of an introduction is normally confined to the first bars of a movement. The irresistible urge of the first subject of the *Allegro* allows no time for the other subjects to expand and develop; its flood sweeps all before it. Everything in this *serenade* seems to violate custom or to break a rule; the profound, almost tragic character of grief with no hope of consolation gives the *Andante* (in D minor) an atmosphere corresponding to nothing in the usual *Andantes* of the *serenades*. One might ask here if Mozart is not bidding farewell to some friendship, some deep emotion of long standing; and this suggestion seems confirmed by the 'Posthorn' calls in the trio of the following minuet.[35]

The Concerto which it was customary to intercalate in these *serenades* is here a *Sinfonia Concertante* (for two flutes, two oboes, two bassoons), clearly a souvenir of the work written on his arrival in Paris, and in which we meet once again the cordial and intimate Salzburg spirit. It must not be forgotten that we are now in fact in the prime of the *Sinfonia concertante*, and that we must wait until Mozart arrives in Vienna before he writes a true concerto for a solo instrument. Until then his practice will be to group together diverse 'solo' instruments, as he did in Paris and Mannheim; and these groupings, as far as the orchestral part is concerned, give rise to real symphonic works that could not be omitted in an historical review of Mozart's symphonies.[36]

So we find that the *Sinfonia concertante* for violin and viola:
*56—K.364:

Allegro maestoso

---

[35] Abert, vol. i, p. 811.

[36] The great piano concertos of his maturity would themselves deserve study from a purely symphonic point of view.

written towards the end of 1779 is comparable in proportions to the quartet *concertante* of Paris, and just as 'Mannheimist' in treatment. Mozart here definitely returns to a taste long appreciated in his own country; he gives us a sort of dialogue, or grand *duo*, between two instruments which are almost the personification of the two performers. The orchestra is really imposing, with its long train of trills in the 'cellos, beneath *tremolando* strings, and its fixed tonality (E flat); it is persistently 'Mannheimist', and one could readily believe it intended for some of the Mannheim virtuosi, Fränzl or Eck for example, rather than the ordinary run of players at Salzburg. Moreover, we do not know the occasion that called forth this great work. It is noble and passionate, and it is not difficult to see in it an anticipation of several of the works of the master's maturity in the same key, E flat, which are analogous in feeling with this work—for different keys represented for Mozart particular modes of poetic expression. The plaintive and sombre *Andante* is a sort of elegy, the *sordini* as it were stifling the sobs; it is one of those painful, even poignant moments, that are far from rare in Mozart. The inspiration is akin to, though much sadder than, that of the preceding *Andante*—that of the great *serenade* composed in August. Thus everything leads us to believe that the *concertante* dates from the following autumn. As for the finale, it is a quick movement well calculated to dispel the shades so lately all around us.[37]

One might almost call the present, the symphonic period of Mozart's life: the period of the *Sinfonia concertante*. In fact, the effect of all that he had learnt at Mannheim or Paris was chiefly a stressing of some one instrument, or category of instruments, in the ensemble. And then the opportunity to write for a whole series of eminent soloists tended to emphasize the *concerto* spirit which shows itself in a variety of manners, in a variety

[37] This period, the heyday of the *Sinfonia concertante*, gave us another work of Mozart, unfinished; it is the opening portion, fairly extensive, of a similar symphony for violin, viola and 'cello, in A (K. Supplement 104). It is scored for the same orchestra as the *concertante* for violin and viola.

of instrumental groupings. Later, all will be used; the musical ensemble will absorb technical innovations and once more the development of instrumental virtuosity will be found to have made a notable contribution, to have enriched and enlarged the whole field of music.

The present period closes with a work that has points of resemblance to that which opened it, that is to say, the symphony in G. The resemblance is particularly in the heroic character of its first movement: it is a symphony in C major:

*57—K.338.

with all the qualities associated with this key. Finished on August 29th 1780, one can already imagine Mozart thinking in the heroic accents of *Idomeneo*; the symphony opens with an imposing vigour in the clear and almost bare tonality of C major, but almost immediately there are romantic nuances to colour and vary the picture. There are sudden alternations of major and minor, a multitude of themes, and a romantic development of a novel character which, in spite of that, is linked to the first part in unaccountable fashion. The concluding *pianissimo* produces something of the same effect as the end of the development of the great E flat symphony (1788): as in the preceding symphonies this first movement has no repeats, but is built rather in the manner of an overture; it ends with an almost triumphal *Coda* on the proud and martial first subject. The whole is primarily heroic and brilliant: but how strongly one feels that Mozart was scarcely ever capable of writing a movement simply and solely heroic and brilliant! This movement is strewn with contrasts resulting from abrupt modulations; and then the unexpected nature of the development gives quite a modern impression, fleetingly almost 'Schumannesque'.

It is hard to understand how this work has until quite lately impressed solely by its superficial character, and how the novelty and variety of its nuances remain still unperceived.

It is particularly difficult for us to express our thoughts concerning the *Andante di molto*, scored for strings with the addition of a solitary flute. There are short moments in life which defy explanation, it may be because their unexpected variety remains untranslatable, or rather because their brevity and charm have a unique character, that is to say which never reappear. It is a question of something indefinite, but of which one feels any return or revival is impossible. Well, it is such a moment as this, in its apparent simplicity, that reveals this *Andante* to us, with a delicacy and emotion we have never paralleled even in the work of Mozart.

The symphony included a minuet which was never completed, and which Mozart suppressed.[38] As for the finale, it has an energy and fire which sets it apart in the master's symphonic work; it suggests a sort of tarantelle carrying all before it in its passionate *élan*. The themes are diversified, but never interrupt this lively rhythm; on the contrary, each seems to supplement the other, to give still more force to the whole movement. In one of his letters Mozart tells us he had to direct this symphony: 'It went *magnifique*. There were forty violins'.[39] We see from this that Mozart was not dismayed by an orchestral mass, and that his symphonies were designed for large combinations of instruments. This one marks, from the symphonic standpoint, the onset of his full mastery, to be more and more rapidly accentuated during the few years of his glorious and brief maturity.

If we now enquire what were Mozart's varied tendencies during this period, we must recognise that the French influence is in general the dominant one, despite the Viennese style and

[38] The original manuscript of the symphony belongs today to the Library of the Paris Conservatoire, from the Malherbe bequest.

[39] Mozart's Letters, 11th April 1781. See *Letters of Mozart and his Family*, tr. Anderson, vol. iii, page 1076. Mozart adds, 'the wind instruments were all doubled, there were ten violas, ten double basses, eight violoncellos and six bassoons.' (But see also Tovey, *Essays in Musical Analysis*, vol. i, page 181). (Tr.)

the survival of the Italian form. Sometimes, too, the master seems to draw near to Haydn—but at the same time decidedly following his own bent, and we feel from now on that Mozart's genius is already so sure of itself, so powerful, that he can be content to borrow a procedure or a form from one or the other, but that his language and technique are now definitely formed, that the unshakeable foundations of this language are already laid.

This period of mellowing and deepening, spent entirely in the calm of Salzburg, gave him the opportunity to absorb and fuse for ever in one crucible all the new instrumental devices, all the impressions gained in Mannheim and Paris. He is to turn them to account and give us the true meaning and right application in the tragedy *Idomeneo*, already in his head; this is the goal to which all the striving, all the experiments, in a nutshell, all the riches and inventions gained from the most memorable of all his travels are leading.

CHAPTER ELEVEN

Vienna (1781-1786)

Symphony-serenade in D (K.385) 1782
Symphony in C, the 'Linz' (K.425) 1783
Funeral Ode (K.477) 1785

MORE THAN A YEAR after he finally settled in Vienna[40] Mozart made the acquaintance of a rich amateur, Baron van Swieten, through whom he gradually came to know and understand the principal masterpieces of the old masters. Not only did van Swieten implant an admiration for Bach and Handel that was to last to the end of his days, but charged him with the thankless task of 're-orchestrating' several of the latter's most celebrated works. Mozart was also expected to take part in performances at the house of his new patron; he had to direct many a choral or instrumental work of Handel or Bach, and no more was needed to make him an immediate convert to these two great men. The moment had arrived when counterpoint and fugue were to give rise to numerous attempts at elaboration and rejuvenation; and while their beauty is revived in him, counterpoint and fugue become his favourite modes of expression. His contrapuntal haste and fever is so great that a number of works remain unfinished, and looking over them one cannot help bitterly regretting this incomplete state. Moreover, another revelation, equally important artistically, led to a fresh conception of Rondo form and incited him to throw off some admirable fantasias, which show him freely

[40] Mozart arrived in Vienna on 16th March 1781, having been summoned there from Salzburg by the Archbishop. (Tr.)

improvising at the piano; a result, this, of reading Emanuel Bach, which we can also attribute to the new intimacy with van Swieten. One can see how during this period of his life he was leaving Viennese taste behind him, and can realise the value for him of this enthusiastic study of great classical music.

In the symphonic field this double, illustrious and salutary influence revealed itself on the eve of the production of *Il Seraglio* in a totally unexpected manner. Mozart, overburdened with work, receives an urgent command from Salzburg: it is the end of July 1782, and the Haffner family are imploring another symphony to add to the brilliance of the family gathering.[41] Mozart hastily sets to work (20th July 1782).

But what changes! What will his fellow-townsmen say to this? The opening of his new symphony-serenade (K.385):

*58

Allegro con spirito

with no prelude (save the indispensable march[42]) presents us with a long and severe, even aggressive theme, which is going to occupy the whole movement, with only a few interruptions by rapid *ritornelli*. There is no second subject. The movement is a *fugato* in which harsh and incisive seconds succeed each other with but little respite. We are several hundred leagues from the brilliant and flowing movements we are accustomed to hear in the shades of Salzburg . . . But the master had forgotten these times. He could not bring himself straight from the pages of Bach or Handel back to the old charming and facile manner so much in vogue in his native town. So he presents the respectable burghers of his own land with one of the most audacious works ever entrusted by him to an orchestra: audacious

[41] The occasion was the ennobling of Siegmund Haffner, Elisabeth Haffner's brother. (Tr.)

[42] K.408, No. 2. (Tr.)

Franz Count Esterházy von Galanta
Mezzotint after a painting by F. Balko by J. G. Haid, Vienna 1769

first, in its archaic style highly spiced with the harmonic tang with which Mozart so often offends the somewhat amorphous palate of his contemporaries; second, by the unique subject that provides the substance of the piece. This is, indeed, something quite exceptional, something Mozart himself has never dared risk in a true symphony. And see too what infinite variety is imposed on this theme by modulations of a boldness unsurpassed or even unapproached by anyone of his epoch. Those of the development, in particular, are so hazardous that it is surprising that they have passed without protest from ignoramuses or pedants; these might well have given rise to the very ungracious sort of criticism that has been provoked by the first bars of the last of the six quartets dedicated to Joseph Haydn.

The first movement is in Sonata Form, despite its contrapuntal character; though deprived of repeat marks, one can see quite clearly where they would be, viz., after a symphonic *ritornello* such as can be found elsewhere in other symphonies of Mozart, leading to the dominant. So here we behold an important work, to open one of the richest periods in Mozart's life; everything in this life presents a sort of harmony, and one cannot forbear to observe that if the Vienna period opens, in the symphonic field, with this unexpected homage to the language of the old masters, it will likewise end with a composition which is as it were the apotheosis of counterpoint and fugue, the final goal of all his instrumental career revivified by a return to all that is greatest and most solid in the past, and what has already been called Mozart's symphonic testament: the finale of his last, the 'Jupiter' symphony.

The rest of this *Haffner-Musik*, particularly the *Andante* and the minuet—there had originally been a second, suppressed when this symphony-serenade was performed in 1783 at one of his Viennese concerts—is much more in keeping with the original purpose of the music and needs no special comment; but the finale has a verve and animation which it is no exaggeration to say approaches that of the *Figaro* overture. We sense here, from the very beginning, a clear reminder of the recent *Il Seraglio*, a sketch of the terror and buffoonery of Osmin; the life, spirit and energy of this finale make it a work of a delicacy and fervour without precedent. Towards the end a sort of *Coda* adds to the unexpectedness; it is impossible at this point of exultation and ecstasy not to be reminded of Joseph Haydn and his habit of redoubling the gaiety of his finales towards the end.

It is clear that at this particular moment of his sojourn in Vienna Mozart had no other model so far as the orchestra was concerned, and it must be stated once more that Haydn was then reigning in Vienna with almost unrivalled glory. Moreover, 1782 was the year in which the younger master set to work composing the first of the six quartets, to be offered three years later to his illustrious *confrère* and elder; so his ears would certainly, and very naturally, be full of Haydn's latest compositions. And the relations between the two great men had become, or were about to become, much more cordial; Leopold Mozart's visit to his son in 1785, and the dedication of the six quartets to Joseph Haydn, helped to reinforce the existing bonds, and to make Haydn's influence much more noticeable; while for the same reason Mozart's influence on Haydn continued to grow.

It is the general opinion that in the C major symphony (K.425):

*59

composed at Linz and dated 3rd November 1783 the acme of Haydn's influence is reached. The character of the introductory *Adagio*, the theme and the march rhythms of the succeeding *Allegro spirituoso*, the development section of the final *Presto*, etc., are instanced as direct reflections of the art of the Esterház master. It is certain that this symphony, which

truly opens the period of Mozart's great orchestral compositions, is akin to Haydn's symphonies in certain obvious ways,
if one wished to find an absolute model for it—notably in the
prevailing mood of the finale, and also in the working out of
the development of this entrancing movement. All this is
indisputable. But to our mind Mozart's individuality is so over-
whelmingly apparent in the symphony as a whole that it is
scarcely possible, at this stage of his growth, to imagine any
inspiration from without; to Mozart, and to Mozart alone,
belong the varied shades of feeling in the first movement—
nuances often attributable to the well-managed use of contrast
between wind and strings; his, too, is the march that runs
through this movement, at once warlike and dreamy. And to
what, if not the profound genius of Mozart, do we owe the
wonderful and touching beauty of the *Poco Adagio*? The
sombre clouds that momentarily tarnish its pure and serene
inspiration neither form nor dissolve in the manner of Haydn;
in its complexity it is already the grand *Adagio* of the classical
symphony in which one feels that the last word has been said.
It is certainly not easy to understand how Mozart, taken un-
prepared by old Count Thun on his arrival at Linz, could in
the space of a few short days have accomplished such a feat;
it seems likely that the conception of the symphony was an
accomplished fact before he left Salzburg, where he had just
spent a holiday, and that he had to do no more than write it
down some time between his departure and his return.

The minuet is one of the most celebrated; one is liable to
find it anywhere. We have seen it figuring in what is called the
'Ballet' in *Don Giovanni*, and in the short dances in *Figaro* . . .
The fact is, it is more suitable for dancing than symphonic
minuets in general are; and even in the *trio*, also in C major, its
charming, soft light is maintained; the way the theme of this *trio*
is taken up in imitation is unrivalled in any similar passage of
Mozart. As for the finale, we willingly concede that the shadow
of the great Haydn is discernible; but we must add at once that
the variety of emotions and the undercurrent of passionate uneasiness give it so 'Mozartian' a quality as soon as the composer

83

gets into his subject that the very intention of following a model is effaced, and all previous suggestions become subject to an inner world of his own. It cannot be denied, however, that the treatment of the development section and the rapid passages preceding the ends of both parts derive from Haydn; these passages apart, the whole symphony stands as a pure and noble creation of Mozart, now in the full bloom of his maturity.

If, moreover, the chronological list of Haydn's symphonies is examined with any care one cannot but be struck by the very small number of those dated between 1780 and 1782 whose introduction gives rise to a slow movement, and in general the symphonies of the Esterház master scarcely show any clear points of comparison with the Linz symphony before those that he wrote for Paris and London.[43] In comparing the Linz symphony with Haydn's works no one has envisaged the much more probable case of the reaction of this symphony on the elder composer's art. And frankly, who knows to what ideals the young master was wedded, in the autumn of this year, 1783? When he returned to Vienna and had to write this symphony in C major on his Linz visit he most certainly had with him a symphony by his old master and Salzburg friend, Michael Haydn who, delighted to meet his erstwhile pupil again, gave him, as a souvenir of past times, one of his latest symphonies, written in the spring of the same year. Until recent times this symphony was attributed to Mozart, who had taken the trouble to copy out the parts himself with a view to its performance at one of his Vienna concerts, or perhaps even at Linz to meet the immediate needs of a concert organised by Count Thun, the dedicatee of the symphony in C we are dealing with. At this period in his artistic career Mozart seems to have regarded a slow introduction as almost indispensable for the opening of a grand symphony; and in fact he wrote an *Adagio* to serve as an introduction to this symphony of Michael Haydn; the result is that people have believed themselves faced with an authentic Mozart symphony! The

[43] See the catalogue which heads the great Breitkopf Edition of Haydn's symphonies.

symphony in question is that in G bearing the number 444 of Köchel's catalogue:[44]

*60   Adagio maestoso

It is difficult to comprehend how the editors of the great Breitkopf Edition could have considered the three movements of the G major symphony as the immediate successors of the 'Linz' symphony; the infinitely simpler and more archaic art of the Salzburg master offers such a contrast that one might well suppose this symphony to date much earlier than 1783, actually the year of its birth. But the important point to note is this choice of Mozart, for whom the instrumental work of his old master had retained its value and importance. It proves in what high esteem Mozart held him; and up to the present no one has discovered any composition by Joseph Haydn that he has taken the trouble not only to copy out in his own hand but in addition to adorn with an expressive prelude which, moreover, is by no means entirely in key with the movement it is intended to prepare.

. . . . .

Two years elapsed before an unexpected event occurred, offering Mozart the opportunity of writing, not a new symphony, but a short funeral ode to the memory of two brother free-masons: Duke Georges-Auguste de Mecklenburg-Strelitz and Count François Esterházy de Galanta, (November 1785)(K.477):

*61

[44] K. (3rd ed.) 425a (Tr.)

this is a short movement of the utmost significance. The composition of the orchestra is itself peculiar; besides the string quartet it includes two oboes, one clarinet, two horns, three bassett horns and a double bassoon. Around a Canto Fermo of liturgical origin the orchestra weaves arabesques with a most modern effect; harmonies to be met again only in the first pages of the *Requiem* rend the noble meditation of the opening; then comes a march rhythm depicting almost visibly the double funeral, accompanying the Canto Fermo. When the *cortège* arrives there breaks out a note of agony which, in due course, is expressed only in short sobs, more and more widely spaced, leading to a dull resignation quenched at last in a final major chord, *pianissimo*. This spirit of profound resignation, free from all revolt, and likewise far removed from any weakness in the face of death, reveals the very depths of Mozart's confident and Christian soul.

This funeral ode, despite its brevity, is a symphony. It remains almost completely unknown; nevertheless, as much by its instrumental treatment as by its psychological insight, it is one of the most important moments Mozart ever experienced. And it provides the occasion to repeat that the use of wind instruments here reaches heights that are still unsuspected. Mozart, as far back as 1785, using similar resources, has here written an instrumental prelude to his *Requiem*.

CHAPTER TWELVE

The Prague Symphony (6th December 1786)

*62—K.504.

SOME MONTHS AFTER THE *Marriage of Figaro* Mozart entered on a period of artistic growth which was to yield fruits so numerous and so rich that it is astonishing to see the majority of biographies so little impressed with the fact. Both the expression and the form of his work will grow and intensify; they will give to his work a range infinitely greater and higher, with more force and bolder relief; and we can say that this period, closing with *Don Giovanni* and the great symphonies, marks the most truly 'romantic' epoch of his career. For freedom, originality and poetry it compares with that of his last visit to Italy, in 1773, with the addition, naturally, of the ripening of a genius which has attained, or is shortly to attain, its fullest radiance. But to reach the middle of this period Mozart must go through some months of transition when, perhaps under the influence of a man too unjustly disdained by him, Muzio Clementi, he will be striving to elaborate long movements built on a single subject, uniting consummate science with the divine fire of his genius. It is particularly noteworthy that, in this transitory period, it is principally the works for piano that benefit by this newly acquired power, which makes it all the more probable that the Italian master's influence was then acting on him with peculiar force. The piano sonatas, trios and concertos particularly show this sort of progress, visible, one might say, at a very first glance.

It was at the end of these few months that he had to write, for an occasion that has remained unknown, the symphony in D (K.504) known as the *Prague Symphony*.[45] It would seem that everything Mozart intended for the inhabitants and connoisseurs of that city was invested with a quite peculiar fire and animation; he felt almost certain of being thoroughly and profoundly understood there. And this is no small encouragement to the artist, nor is it less a merit in those who bring it about. We know, too, in what enthusiastic terms he spoke of his Prague friends after *Don Giovanni*.

His first knock on their door was with the symphony in D, re-echoing with a rough, a solid assurance. The success was equal to its anticipation. In listening to this symphony one has sometimes, nay often, the impression of being in the presence of Beethoven, so closely are the grandeur of design and the vigour with which it is realised bound together; that enormous prelude with its intensifying rising phrases, and the modulations of the little *'gruppetti' motif*, herald events so solemn that one is almost astonished on hearing the principal theme of the *Allegro*, passionately 'modern' in character, its feverish syncopations contrasting with the heroic interruptions from the brass. One has a striking impression of novelty, as much in the inspiration as in the scoring and harmony of all this movement. Mozart here no longer speaks the language we have met in his former compositions; we get the impression that this language is entirely his own creation, and we know of no musician who might have been able to reveal its elements to him. Perhaps if we were forced to choose one the name of Clementi would again present itself most readily to our mind. We have a foreshadowing of the *Magic Flute*, not only in the cast of the ideas themselves but in the effects obtained by means of counterpoint; and this symphony would be memorable if only from

---

[45] The first edition of this symphony, by André of Offenbach (Op. 87), was advertised in July 1801 (*Allgemeine Musikalische-Zeitung*).

his point of view. The whole of the development is significant in this respect and, we would say, unique as a precursor of things to come; and the way in which the recapitulation is modulated and varied is also absolutely characteristic in its astonishing modernism. The romantic criticism of Mozart which sees in him nothing but an Olympic god, eternally serene, never experiencing the troubles or anxieties of mortal uneasiness, seems to us quite incomprehensible, the more so since this D major symphony is by no means an isolated phenomenon in his work.

Another matter for surprise awaits us in this first movement, which we might readily expect to see built entirely on the first subject, followed by rhythmic figures on the brass and vigorous contrapuntal designs; it is the presence, nevertheless, of a second subject, but relegated to the very end of the first part, and then quickly hurried through. Mozart, after some months during which, probably under Clementi's influence, he schooled himself to build his first *Allegros* on a single subject, returned gradually to the contrast of two subjects; and thus the D major symphony clearly marks the end of the transition period we mentioned above.

It would be difficult to employ chromaticisms and counterpoint with a more constant subtlety than in the *Andante* (in G major), in which feelings of such variety are so intermingled that a new and enchanted world seems to open before our eyes for the first time. We feel ourselves quite powerless to describe it; we recognise in this marvellous and most musical reverie something pastoral or idyllic; but for all the singing of birds and the murmuring of waters, fleeting clouds often come to darken the landscape. There are sometimes even cries of anguish to be heard; but nature's all-pervading peace soon regains the mastery, and, despite most intense and modern dissonances, despite modulations which vary the first subject at each repetition during the development, the movement ends on a note of inward peace, of poetic repose. Perhaps it is permissible to find here something akin to the feeling, not easily definable, that emerges from the 'Scene by the brook', a feeling that only the very

89

greatest poets have been able to suggest; and it is certainl
not the much-vaunted simplicity of Mozart that reigns her
This movement proves the richness and variety of his inne
life; it also proves him to have been intensely moved by th
most intimate and subtle poetry of nature.

The finale, whose initial rhythm recalls the short duet i
Figaro where Cherubino escapes by jumping through
window, is, like the other two movements, built with th
rigorous symmetry of Sonata Form. To our mind, whateve
one may say, it is again one wherein joy is not unalloyed;
burning, ardent passion creeps in and, despite its opening, it i
rather of the ardours of the almost contemporary *Don Giovann*
that this finale reminds us . . . There are, moreover, certai
aspects in which this symphony is akin to the famous overtur
to *Don Giovanni*. Elements of drama and joy are, in fact, closel
intermingled; the symphony certainly ends on the latter not
but on some abrupt, almost lacerating rhythms that sugges
more of struggle and energy than of real happiness. We do no
know what hindered Mozart from writing a minuet for thi
symphony; perhaps the total exclusion of dancing is deliberat
or, in any case, more usual in Prague than in Vienna.

CHAPTER THIRTEEN

A Musical Joke; or A Symphonic Caricature (14th June 1787)

*63—K.522.

THIS WORK, OFTEN DESIGNATED 'The Village Musicians' or 'Peasant Symphony' is actually entitled 'A musical Joke' (*Ein musikalischer Spass*). It is thus headed by Mozart himself in the catalogue of his works.

Everyone seems to have been totally mistaken as to the real idea behind this parody, and Herr Hermann Abert, the greatest modern biographer of Mozart, opens up new avenues in this connection in the second volume of his remarkable work.[46] What has until now been taken for a satire on the playing of poor and unskilled musicians is really directed much more against the infatuated ignorance of the composer aspiring to write something resembling—however faintly—a symphony. It is not the deliberately falsified cadences or passages that 'misfire' which ought to attract our attention so much as the grotesque emptiness and the only too obvious incompetence of the so-called composer. Most assuredly Mozart must have had some 'model' in writing this curious work, and we can certainly speak of influence here though we do not know the person aimed at!

[46] Hermann Abert, *W. A. Mozart*, vol. ii, pp. 394 *et seq.*

He adopts the older symphonic framework, using strings and two horns; or rather, he was thinking of the *Divertimento*, then very much the fashion in Vienna since it gave many a composer the chance of a quick popularity. These works were heard in the *salons*, also in the open air in fine weather, so that opportunity for them to become known was not lacking.

The most striking thing about this parody of a symphony is the fundamental incapacity of the composer to bind two ideas together in any logical sequence whatever; this incapacity is such that, in the first movement particularly (for the *Plaisanterie* includes four movements in the style of a true symphony) there are whole passages with merely an accompaniment droning away in the basses and violas, with no additional part to impart sense to this meaningless murmur; and then, even the most elementary sense of modulation invariably fails the composer every time he needs it. Clearly Mozart had not the intention of presenting the insufferable spectacle of a tyro attempting to handle the full orchestra; he has chosen, with impeccable taste, the more modest canvas of the *Divertimento* or sextet with two horns; at the same time the idea is to produce something resembling or even giving the illusion of a symphony such as was still in vogue during Mozart's youth.

The long and ungainly *fioriture* in the slow movement seem to suggest an over-ambitious violinist, but also reveal to us a composer who is prey to the worst sentimentality, endeavouring to interpret it by scrappy bits of tune and excessive digression. The *longueurs* of this movement are perhaps even surpassed by the trio of the minuet, cut to a most unusual pattern; some timid attempts at counterpoint usher in the repeat of the minuet. But the finale is, perhaps, the most remarkable of all; the composer here risks an actual *fugato*, which stops short after four bars, as in fact do most of his ideas. It is a hotch potch of unrelated themes, with no logical order to it; one senses a mind more fertile in the attempt than in the realisation. But we have here a veritable *rondo*, full of a humour at once subtle and coarse, during which the most unexpected things keep happening, notably that attempt at *fugato*, serious and at the

92

me time grotesque. We may ask, with Herr Abert, if the last
nords on the strings, each string in a different key, may not be
nterpreted as a final joke on the part of the performers at the
omposer's expense—who truly, for all he had to say, has
ept them too long occupied.

CHAPTER FOURTEEN

The Final Great Trilogy

Symphony in E flat
Symphony in G minor
Symphony in C (the 'Jupiter')

WHEN ONE CONSIDERS THE level reached by Mozart at t[
time of writing *Don Giovanni* one can say that he h[
there attained the most romantic summit of his entire care[
since his three great symphonies all belong to this same peri[
of artistic effort. *Don Giovanni* was first played at the end [
October 1787, and the three symphonies were finished, one [
26th June 1788, and the others on 25th July and 10th Augu[
of the same year. We could, therefore, put the time of the[
inception in the first half of 1788. It would be not at all diffic[
to instance many a rhythmic or harmonic detail showing t[
three symphonies united to the famous opera by a commo[
inspiration; and the scales that plough through the first pa[
of the overture to the latter make their reappearance, with st[
bolder dissonances, in the spacious introduction to the E f[
symphony, the first of the three.[47]

In bestowing the title 'trilogy' on this famous set of mast[
pieces the suggestion of a bond between them is intention[
this trinity, we may be sure, has not come about by chan[
Never since he arrived at maturity had he produced, at interva[
of a few days only, a succession of compositions of the sa[
calibre; the E flat symphony represents an immense porti[
through which the composer reveals to us all the warm a[

[47] See Abert, *W. A. Mozart*, vol. ii, p. 569.

oetic beauty thronging his mind, before surrendering himself
efore our eyes to a struggle of exalted passion, to be manifest
a the symphony in G minor; and finally he invites our presence
: a sort of apotheosis of his musical genius, freed from all
1ackles, in what has come to be known as the 'Jupiter' sym-
hony. This imposing triple aspect that he gives to his sym-
honic testament in some measure sums up for us his inmost
)ul, and one can well understand that the production of the
rst should be followed so closely by the other two. But one
1rely ought not to imagine that Mozart intended to interpret
1 the vicissitudes he was going through at the time of writing;
1e sorry happenings of his daily round have nothing in com-
1on with the blossoming of his secret soul. And when all is
1id it is to the hidden energy of his genius, more than to any
:her cause, that we must ascribe the creation of those three
1onumental works, dominating as they do his own instrumen-
l work and, we may say, the whole of the instrumental output
: the eighteenth century. As for the external circumstances
tending on their birth, we are in total ignorance; we have not
1e least notion of the orchestra they were intended for,[48] nor
1y other particular detail of their origin or first public perfor-
1ance. We must therefore be content, before embarking upon
1 analysis, with a few critical sketches from France and
'ermany dating from fifteen or twenty years after their com-
letion, that is to say, about the time when the world first
:gan to have some idea of their artistic importance and their
re-eminent beauty.

Mozart's instrumental music, principally his great sym-
1onies, began to make its appearance in France from 1805
1wards, in the programmes of the 'Exercices publics des
èves du Conservatoire', which were then giving place to real
1ncerts, with critical notices.[49] In 1806 a fragment of a Mozart
·mphony was received 'with enthusiasm', and works of this
1aster are so much the fashion that the writer feels obliged to

[48] The dates of the first editions, published by André of Offenbach,
e: 1797, 1794, and 1793. (Tr.)
[49] See *La Décade Philosophique*, from 1805; *Les Tablettes* (1810-1811).

95

press for the more frequent performance of Italian works: 'w
have even', he writes with some indignation, 'had three pieces b
Mozart in the same concert'. On 22nd March 1807 the rehears
of the Conservatoire pupils opened with a performance of
Mozart symphony, played this time in its entirety; and we hav
good reason to believe the symphony in question to have bee
the G minor. 'If the first movement, for example', explains th
writer, 'seems to have less grandeur and, so to say, less amp
proportions (than Haydn), there is more brilliance and lightnes
though the harmony is as skilful and the modulations as bol
There is no *Andante* of Haydn more enjoyable than this one b
Mozart; in the second half a new and quite original figure mak
its appearance on the basses alone, then is taken up by the oth
instruments with modulations, until the basses make use
part of this figure to lead back to the first *motif*. This delightf
theme is so well managed that, though the movement is lon
it seems to end too soon. The two minuets are piquant an
lively; and the final *Presto*, a movement sometimes a bit pe
functory in Haydn's symphonies, is here most charming. It
a *rondeau*,[50] both melodic and at the same time full of spirit an
warmth. This is to dwell rather long on a single symphony; bu
it is the first by this master to be heard at the Conservatoi
for a long time (his overtures are another matter), and what w
said in our last number has tempted us to go into these details.'
On 5th April following a Mozart symphony appeared agai
'The *Andante*, from another symphony, was a superlativ
choice, and made a most pleasing effect. The minuets, in livel
tempo, and the final *Presto* were applauded as warmly as the
were played; and this warmth could only respond to a lik
quality in the composition—a quite extraordinary warmtl
which one finds in all Mozart's best compositions. This maste
seems always to have written with inspiration'.[52]

[50] All instrumental finales were apt to be called *Rondeau*; this part
cular one has no connection with the rondo form.

[51] *La Décade Philosophique*: 2nd Year, to September 1807. Th
critical notices are due to La Chabeaussiere (1752-1820).

[52] Ibid.

96

We cannot unfortunately determine with certainty just which symphony was performed on 19th April 1807, and which seems to absorb the critic in an ever growing interest; perhaps it was the 'Jupiter': 'It is very difficult, full of minute detail, of fleeting passages of imitation, of fine nuances requiring from all the participants rare precision and sustained attention, with no relaxation whatever. This is especially true of the last *Presto*, a brilliant and satisfying movement when perfectly played, but which the least carelessness or inaccuracy would reduce to chaos. Whether it be regarded as a virtue or a vice in Mozart's music, this abundance of detail, of little subjects and countersubjects scattered throughout the orchestra is a characteristic.[53] It is the excess, perhaps the abuse, of a learned style and a fertile imagination. This music, despite its complication, is intelligible and even clear to him who knows how to listen, provided nothing in the execution is lacking; deprived of this degree of precision, so difficult to attain, you will understand nothing'.[54] And the Conservatoire students, on 24th May, gave another performance, 'more glowing and accurate', of the G minor symphony.

From this one can see how the French were struck by their first contact with Mozart's instrumental art, and it can even be said that the critic here shows himself infinitely more comprehensive and acute than when dealing with Mozartian opera, whether *Les Mystères d'Isis* (1801), or *Don Giovanni* (1805). Theorists, too, were not inactive, and the G minor was made the subject of a long critical analysis—or rather corrective, for the author is profoundly shocked by the liberties, particularly in the harmony, that Mozart permits himself—signed J. de Momigny.[55] We shall naturally ignore the corrections which the author, in the name of 'good taste', suggests in almost every bar of the symphony, but retain his aesthetic appreciation of the general character of the first movement, the first subject of

[53] Perhaps, indeed, the fugal finale of the 'Jupiter' is here in question.
[54] Ibid.
[55] Framery et Guinguené, *Encyclopédie méthodique*, vol. iii, art. Symphonie, p. 412 *et seq.* (1818).

which is 'of an impassioned grief'. Likewise in the second part of the finale—that is to say, during the course of the development—we are in the presence of an 'eloquent frenzy of a lost, tormented soul, but perhaps Mozart has counted too much on the intelligence of the players . . .' As for the *Andante*, 'we see there only magnificent accompaniments, and we seek the countenance of this grand and handsome body . . .'

When we compare these pre-romantic criticisms with those of thirty-five years or more ago we can realise the changes that have taken place between our great-grandfathers' generation and that of our fathers, or our own. The G minor symphony towards the end of the nineteenth century is scarcely more than a musical trifle tinged with gentle melancholy. What would have been said then of a writer daring to speak of 'l'éloquent délire' of Mozart? Mozart is invariably Apollo, or at least a Parthenon frieze. And his admirers of twenty or thirty years ago would have been almost grieved had one spoken of the ardent passion, the warm tenderness, which almost every page of Mozart holds for us.

Passing now to German criticism at the beginning of the nineteenth century we encounter some very similar appraisals; as in France it is most often the G minor symphony whose passionate ardour calls forth comment. At the Augarten subscription concerts in Vienna, in existence since Mozart's time, the G minor symphony was heard in 1804: 'this veritable masterpiece where nothing is too long or too short, where all is conducted in the most exact fashion; where everything down to the finest detail contributes to the whole and seems indispensable to the completion of the mighty picture of a mind swayed by passion, ranging from the extremity of grief to the borders of the sublime. However often the work is heard, it never fails in its effect; every time it grips the listener irresistibly and sweeps him along in its train.' [56] Nearly a year later, in May 1805, there is another performance of this amazing symphony at the same concerts . . . 'This symphony which combines the highest beauty with the greatest nobility of inspiration, and,

[56] *Allgemeine Musikalische-Zeitung*, vol. vi (1804), p. 777.

moreover, founders neither in violence nor in *bizarrerie*. It is a colossal canvas preserving the most exquisite proportions; 'a Jupiter from the chisel of a Phidias, inspiring both respect and love'.[57] In another performance during the same year the minuet seems to have been omitted: and the critic exclaims 'what a pity to suppress the terribly beautiful minuet'.[58]

The impression made on all the writers of the time seems to have been one of tragic grandeur, to which we had not been accustomed by romantic criticism. And in 1808 we come across this conclusion: 'This symphony in which the composer tears so powerfully at our heart-strings that they resound interminably.'[59]

The E flat symphony occasions quite a poem from the pen of the critic Apel, and, if the name *Jupiter* intervenes in an unexpected fashion to underline Mozart's last symphony, it is because everyone is agreed in finding in it the apogee of power and grandeur; but it should be noted that, in both France and Germany, criticism becomes more readily expansive over the exalted passion which, for them and ourselves likewise, is the core of the symphony in G minor.[60]

. . . . . .

SYMPHONY IN E FLAT

Completed 26th June, 1788

The scoring consists of strings ('cello and bass parts distinct), one flute, two clarinets, two bassoons, two horns, two trumpets and drums.

---

[57] *Allgemeine Musikalische-Zeitung*, vol. vii, p. 502.
[58] Ibid., p. 613.　　　[59] Ibid., 1808, p. 239.

[60] After the analysis of each of these three great Mozart symphonies we shall continue to give a review of the criticisms they have evoked. Beginning at the end of the eighteenth century we shall run quickly through much of the nineteenth century, ending about 1870, paying more particular attention to the appreciations of such men as Fétis, Hector Berlioz and Richard Wagner.

Immediately following this solemn rhythmic attack a descending scale, in demi-semiquavers, is given to the violins, with an ascending *motif* on the flute, while underneath the timpani maintain a continuous roll. These scales will feature throughout the introduction, and from the violins they pass to the basses where, in contrast, their direction is upwards. And always, beneath these varied scale passages, the persistent, jerky rhythm is maintained, first by the basses, then by the trumpets:

*65

suggesting almost irresistibly an analogous passage in the slow introduction to the *Don Giovanni* overture:

*66

The harmonic boldness of the last bars of the introduction:

*67

gives to the whole of the E flat symphony a romantic character which will be apparent in each of the four movements.

23221

This theme, smooth, warm and sensuous, is followed later by a powerful *ritornello*, with a sort of tzigane rhythm:

*69

then, exactly as in the introduction, descending scales reappear on the violins:

*70

considerably lengthening the *ritornello*. The second subject, in B flat, is divided between the violins and the woodwind:

*71

which, for four bars, are supported simply by the basses; the second part of this second subject itself makes a third subject:

*72

allotted to the strings, accompanied, or punctuated, by double basses *pizzicati*. Then comes a much extended and developed version of the *ritornello* that followed the first subject, fresh modulations making the return of the tzigane rhythm on the violins still more incisive. The end of the first *ritornello* thus serves as a conclusion of the first part of the movement.

After the double bar the development opens with modulations based on the final group of this *ritornello*, giving place to a repeat of the second part of the second subject (Ex.72) in A flat, still with the same *pizzicato* accompaniment. The final group that ushered in the development reappears, giving rise to modulating imitations between basses and first violins; then comes the second subject *ritornello*, varied and modulated. This is arrested on the dominant of C minor; there is a whole bar's silence, then the woodwind alone, in three bars, effects a join (analogous to that at the end of the introduction) with an unexpected modulation.

*73

The recapitulation follows the exposition closely, and the movement ends with a brilliant *Coda*, with no separating repeat marks. The concluding rhythm is very nearly identical with that of the close of the first part.

*74

This theme, which some have found flat and insipid, is going to transport us into unimagined regions, and its faintly martial character hardly prepares us for all the vicissitudes, fierce or gentle, that will arise from its development.

Note first, that it is presented by the strings alone, 'cellos quite distinct from the double basses—thus helping to give the whole movement a romantic character, a modern flavour. The theme is binary in form; it is furnished with repeat marks and a recapitulation, but on its last appearance there is a modulation to the minor. After another double barline the woodwind, as in the first movement, provide a link to the first episode (in F minor). This:

*75

is almost explosive in its energy and abruptness, as Mozart's minor episodes very often are; during the course of this episode the first subject somewhat unexpectedly reappears, in imitation between bassoons and horns on the one hand, and violas and basses on the other. The ascending rhythm of the first subject continues in the bass, slurred, while the violins are concerned with a detached, descending figure, *forte*, in opposition. A remarkable transition, in the first violins, leads to a third subject or episode, *piano*, on the woodwind accompanied by the violins:

*76

This third subject is repeated, in imitations between flutes, clarinets and bassoons, supported by a sustained chord on the horns. The return of the initial theme then follows, but from the fifth bar it passes to the woodwind, violins weaving an expressive counter-melody around it; then the basses and first violins divide the theme between them, with descending scales on the woodwind. The latter then take charge of the theme, while the violins again adorn it with the counter-melody just mentioned; and the minor version of the theme leads, by a marvellous modulation, to the key of B major and the repeat of the first episode, more energetic than ever, this time in B minor. This *reprise* is extended by some new modulations, as expressive as they are unexpected, testifying to a sort of romantic exaltation; the other themes follow in their appropriate order, and then comes a fine *Coda* on the principal theme, initiated by antiphony between woodwind and strings; and the movement, after some expressive and languorous chromaticisms, comes to an end on two chords, *forte*, by the whole orchestra.

*77

This minuet, the most popular of all in Mozart's works, seems to spring from a single idea; and rhythms from the development section of the first movement will be clearly heard. It deploys the full orchestra, and its lively and energetic movement is pursued in one single sweep to the end. The customary contrast arises from the quiet tenderness of the trio:

*78

in the same key; the first clarinet states the theme to the accompaniment of the second, to which the flute replies with a delicate echo. This trio, quite German or Austrian in character, belongs to the same *genre* as Mozart's last German dances, a *genre* very similar to that adopted by Schubert in his Waltzes and Ländler. The trio might well figure in one of the many dance suites composed by Mozart between 1788 and 1791, for the balls and assemblies of Vienna. The compositions his duties obliged him to provide gave him the opportunity to crowd these little pieces, alas, too little known, with gems of orchestration belonging essentially to the symphony. The study of these orchestral suites even throws a new light on the symphonic art of the master, now nearing the end of his short life.

*79

The first violins alone state the theme, accompanied by the seconds. Then the whole orchestra attacks the theme, quickly followed by long roulades, brilliant and gay, on the violins, carried on through a whole page of the score, leading to a fanfare-like cadence in F major. This separates the first period of the second subject, which is itself none other than a return to the first subject—but how varied! The sly and melancholy response of the woodwind is succeeded by modulations becoming more and more audacious and distant, the fanfare rhythms are renewed, and everything halts abruptly on a chord of the six-four. It might be imagined that the *ritornello* ended there; but now the woodwind become involved in some rapid imitations based on the opening of the first subject, and the first half of the movement comes to an end with a loud and joyous *ritornello*, in B flat, on the fanfare rhythm we have previously noted. At the double bar it becomes apparent that the rhythm of the first subject is going to be pursued throughout the whole of this remarkable finale; Mozart, in fact, here returns to the principle of construction he had adopted in 1786. He built his instrumental movements on a single theme, reserving the right to treat and vary it at his pleasure. So at the double bar the strings attack the first notes of the main theme, in unison, in the dominant of C minor, with all the roughness usual with Mozart when he goes into the minor key. But a

bar's rest modifies to some extent the violence of this opening of
the development; the theme appears in the violins exactly as at
the beginning of the movement, but this time in A flat. The
first bars of the theme give rise to an extraordinary development which maintains its rhythm throughout, while the theme
is made to pass through inspired modulations beginning in the
most distant key (E major); it is exchanged between first violins
and basses during nine bars, and then, with imitations at a
closer interval in the same bar, the first and second violins
range themselves against the violas and basses. The contest is
so exhausting that the theme disintegrates, after a violent
unison in G; the fragments continue to appear in the violins,
while the woodwind are busy right up to the recapitulation,
with phrases that defy description:

*80

The latter is regular, with thirteen bars of frenzied *Coda* ending,
à la Haydn, with the initial rhythm of the movement.

. . . . .

Everyone is agreed in recognizing, in this symphony, as it
were the full flowering of the happiness an artist feels in
creation. However, it seems to us that there are plenty of signs
of trouble and uneasiness; the spontaneous audacity of the
harmonies Mozart piles up in the introduction, above the dull
murmur of those pregnant scale passages, is scarcely a fitting
prelude to a cloudless day. For us, this introduction stands at
the threshold of a new era; it has a dominating grandeur
presaging Beethoven;[61] there is, in Haydn at least, no parallel
symphonic opening. It is a new starting point, and being something tremendous said for the first time cannot fail to excite

[61] See Abert, *W.A. Mozart*, vol. ii, p. 568 *et seq.*, where he speaks of
'profound pessimism.'

some measure of astonishment. Mozart, as we have already remarked, here recaptures very fleetingly the accents of his *Don Giovanni* overture; nor will this be the sole instance in the three symphonies when we shall experience his brusque boldness. Then, the *Allegro* theme comes rather as a relief after the heavy atmosphere of the prelude. It is the *cantabile* type of *Allegro* frequent in Mozart, and very characteristic of him. But its division between strings and woodwind, its soft, shaded light, peculiar to the key of E flat, the advantage derived from the use of the clarinet, all go to produce an astonishingly novel effect and—if we add to this a gypsy touch—an impression quite unknown in the music of the time; we have no hesitation in labelling it with that overworked term, 'romantic'. The development, it is true, has nothing of the fullness it will acquire in the remaining two symphonies; but the contrast provoked by the opposition and the key changes of the three subjects accentuates the romantic character of the work. Counterpoint does not here play the preponderant *rôle* we are accustomed to in the classical symphony; but the composer includes in the development nothing that is not strictly thematic and—a new proof of the aesthetic and expressive importance of key in Mozart's work— there are to be found, towards the end, some characteristic effects exactly similar to those in the development section of his famous piano concerto in C minor (first movement), produced by the same means, and by modulation to the same keys.

All through the symphony the harmonic aspect should stand out in relief, since this is largely instrumental in giving a romantic feeling and attitude to the whole. At the moment towards the end of the development when the whole orchestra comes to rest on a pause, followed by the woodwind link passage built on sevenths and ninths, we are in the presence of innovations probably without precedent; and this procedure not only appears new, but was so intended by the composer, since the introduction is joined to the *Allegro* by similar means. And it would not be difficult to instance other harmonic audacities in the *Andante* and the finale.

This *Andante* exhibits a curious peculiarity in the choice of the key of A flat. The choice is romantic in itself; and the un-expected sequence of the episodes unfolded therein makes it a movement unique of its kind. But, once more confirming our thesis of the importance of key to Mozart, we find the same harmonic surprises, if not the same inspiration, in the extra-ordinary *Adagio* that forms the second movement of a sonata in E flat, for piano and violin, composed by Mozart towards the end of 1785.[62] We must expect every kind of surprise when Mozart leads us into the almost forbidden territory of A flat. In the *Andante* under discussion, when the theme sounds in the principal key it awakens in us grave and calm echoes, almost always veiled; but this mysterious region does not remain unchanged; it is sometimes illuminated as by a lightning flash, returning to its former state only after heavy and plaintive lamentations. There is nothing more expressive than this return after the furious outburst of the first episode; the elegiac and tender intimacy of the whole movement is fully revealed only after the various episodes, when in the *Coda* the first theme becomes even more penetrating, its expression more touching and intense. Its sway is exerted more especially in the chro-maticisms, which in one or two bars give a greater poignancy to the principal subject, without destroying the slightly repress-ed character that persists almost throughout the *Andante*. All this is very complex, and even the two almost cruel chords ending the movement provide a new matter for astonishment; for everything had seemed to point to a quiet ending to this elegy, despite the sharply energetic outbursts running through it.

The finale has more surprises prepared for us, of which we are scarcely forewarned by its sprightly and good-natured theme. This, as we have already said, comprises the one and only subject of the movement; more marvellous still, out of it Mozart builds a world whose significance I have no hesitation in saying is, if not greater, at least more original than that of the first movement. One can find many passages having sym-metrical equivalents in the first movement (a fact that gives to

[62] K.481. The *Adagio* of the string trio in E flat, nearly contempo-raneous with the symphony, could also be quoted for its boldness.

108

many of Mozart's works such a complete unity), and especially some enharmonic modulations which, with the changing colour of a single note, open up a new world,[63] a procedure and result essentially romantic. Then there is the truly ineffable passage preceding the recapitulation, when the theme crumbles and disintegrates after its struggle with itself, while the wood-wind, in keys as remote as possible, transport us towards the unknown regions. In truth, here is not 'woodwind', but the wind itself,[64] a murmuring breeze, a zephyr from so distant a poetry that it defies description! The general exuberance with which this finale overflows (reminding us of Haydn) is not all, for Mozart has such a strong tendency towards poetic fantasy that he finds the opportunity, always and everywhere, even in the midst of the most boisterous festivities, to insinuate some-thing of a self-revelatory nature, charged with tenderness and emotion.[65]

. . . . .

The learned Fétis, two years after the inauguration of his *Revue Musicale*, gives an account (27th April 1828),[66] of a concert 'composed entirely of the works of Mozart'.

'The symphony which was chosen to open the first part was the E flat. It contains much beauty, particularly in the *Adagio* and the finale; but I must confess I felt some astonishment at seeing it preferred to the G minor, that beautiful and passion-ate composition! The latter was deemed too well known; but the overture to the *Magic Flute* is still more so, and we saw the effect that produced. The E flat symphony has not the brilliance we expect, after the grand effects of Beet-hoven's symphonies. There are no parts for the oboes, because at the time Mozart wrote it oboists played in that key only with considerable difficulty, regarding it as too difficult. I do not

[63] See for example, the change from A flat to E major, in the develop-ment.

[64] 'ce ne sont plus des "vents", mais le vent.'

[65] The sketch of another symphony in E flat also begins with a slow introduction. (K. supplement, No. 100.)

[66] *Revue Musicale*, p. 318.

know if the somewhat unfavourable opinion a section of the orchestra had of this work had undermined their morale, but it seemed to me that the performance had less sureness and precision than in other concerts, and even in the remainder of this one.'

The opinion here expressed by Fétis seems to have been modified but little as time went on. In one of the last articles written by the great Berlioz for *La Gazette musicale*, in which he was responsible for concert notices, we find these few hasty lines sufficing to describe the symphony: 'The concert ended with the E flat symphony by Mozart. With the exception of the last movement, truly unworthy of such a master, this symphony by the charm of its melodies seems to surpass by far that by Haydn (no. 30) (?) which we have just quoted. It was however much less applauded!' (13th February 1842).

So the success of this symphony, so intimately 'Mozartian', remained a qualified one. It has neither the passion of the G minor, nor the imposing splendour of the 'Jupiter'; therefore neither public nor critics of the romantic age were capable of being profoundly moved by it. A symphony at that time had perforce to be powerful or mournful throughout. We shall see in due course that certain minuets were barely tolerated. At the same time the caustic and almost clownish wit of many a Haydn finale began to offend the ear profoundly. It is likely that the character of the theme of the finale of the E flat symphony was the cause of the severity of its condemnation; the beauty of the treatment of this unique subject could not compensate for the impression the theme itself produced. What we have noticed as precisely 'romantic' in the course of this symphony, and even in this very finale, was completely overlooked. It is more astonishing that the bold and imposing introduction, stirring up dark depths—an opening on the whole much more impressive and romantic than that of either of the two following symphonies—does not seem to have aroused any comment. Most curiously, this abridged model for the prelude of Beethoven's seventh symphony, with its forceful scales, its already sinister and uneasy harmonies, makes no impression. And it is not the absence of oboes that caused musicians, critics, the public, to have an unfavourable opinion of the E flat symphony, which with the recoil of time we regard as one of those in which Mozart's genius is affirmed with the most original variety, with the most unfettered fancy, and above all with youthful and intense poetry.

Speaking generally, the romantic epoch was satisfied with nothing but enormous ensembles in instrumental music. This megalomania swamped chamber music. Mozart's, wholly scorned, was relegated to programmes of the second order. And Berlioz expressed very clearly the state of mind that obtained right to the end of the century, when he said, apropos of a concert given by the Société des Concerts du Conservatoire, of Beethoven's F major symphony: 'It is colossal. Frankly, however one regards it, it is folly to attempt any comparison between such a symphony and those of Mozart, even the finest; the contest is unequal'.[67]

Some thirty years later another genius illuminates with an astonishing penetration the masterpieces of an art already become classic, and which on this account had to suffer from an inflexible 'tradition', established it is true long after the composer's death. Here is how, early in 1865, Richard Wagner complains with bitterness, in a report addressed to the King of Bavaria, of the absence of any authoritative direction with regard to the interpretation of Mozart's orchestral works in Germany.[68]

'Now, let us imagine some such expressive theme of Mozart's —Mozart, who was intimately acquainted with the noble style of classical Italian singing, whose musical expression derived its very soul from the delicate vibrations, swellings and accents of that style, and who was the first to reproduce the effects of this vocal style, by means of orchestral instruments. Let us imagine such a theme of the master's played neatly and smoothly, by an instrument in the orchestra, without any inflection, or increase or decrease of tone or accent, without the slightest

[67] *Gazette Musicale*, 27th March, 1836.

[68] Richard Wagner, *On a German school of music*. Tr. Dannreuther.

touch of that modification of movement and rhythm so indispensable to good singing—but monotonously enunciated, just as one might pronounce some arithmetical number—and then, let us endeavour to form a conclusion as to the vast difference between the master's original intention, and the impressions thus produced. The dubious value of the veneration of Mozart, professed by our musical traditionalists will then also appear. To show this more distinctly, let us examine a particular case—for example, the first eight bars of the second movement of Mozart's celebrated symphony in E flat. Take this beautiful theme as it appears on paper, with hardly any marks of expression; fancy it played smoothly and complacently, as the score apparently has it—and compare the result with the manner in which a true musician would feel and sing it! How much of Mozart does this theme convey, if played, as in nine cases out of ten it *is* played, in a perfectly colourless and lifeless way? "Poor pen and paper music, without a shadow of soul or sense." '

From all this the significance for Richard Wagner of this E flat symphony, and especially the 'marvellous theme' with which it opens, is plainly to be seen. It is not our purpose here to point the moral for orchestral conductors, but to stress Wagner's choice of this symphonic fragment, out of the whole of Mozart's output, to try to convince us of the necessity of 'singing tone' in rendering Mozart. Previously he had pointed out the almost complete absence of directions in Mozart's symphonies; he assumes that the master must have given them himself by word of mouth in conducting his works, thus making himself better understood to his interpreters.

'But the precise importance of these (expression marks) for the performance of Mozart's instrumental works is obvious. With Mozart the so-called development sections, and the connecting links between the main themes, are frequently rather slight, whereas his musical originality shows to greatest advantage in the vocal character of the melodies. Compared with Haydn's the significance of Mozart's symphonies lies in the extraordinarily expressive vocal character of his instrumen-

Grande
SIMPHONIE
Periodique
a plusieurs instrumens
composée par
W·A·MOZART
Oeuvre=9me

S.C.M.

prix f. 3.

Publiée a Vienne chez Artaria Comp.

54   55

tal themes; it is in this character that we find the explanation of how Mozart, in this branch of music, was a great creator'.[69]

It was not chance, but his own genius, that prompted Wagner's choice of the E flat symphony to illustrate the difference between the performance of this symphony under the direction of an inspired artist, and the indifferent interpretations, colourless and lifeless, giving the impression of 'soulless music', that we are usually offered. The finale seems to him quite as important as the first movement. He sees in it a very eloquent example of those *allegros* wherein the figuration outweighs the melody. 'It is', he adds, 'an orgy of pure rhythm'.[70] These famous words of Wagner apply as much to the finale of Beethoven's seventh symphony as to that of Mozart's E flat; these movements are, for him, equal in value.

This, moreover, is not the first time this similarity has impressed itself on Wagner's mind. In one of the most charming passages from his memoirs, entitled: *Ein glücklicher Abend* we read the following:

' . . . We had, among other lovely things, Mozart's E flat and Beethoven's seventh.

'. . . In my opinion there is always this difference between these two symphonies: in Mozart the language of the heart is breathed in quiet and tender longing, while in the work of his rival this desire is hurled boldly towards the infinite. In Mozart's symphony it is the plenitude of feeling that is uppermost; in Beethoven's, the fearless consciousness of power.

'"How I love", cried my friend, "to hear you thus illumining these sublime orchestral compositions!"'[71]

Quite clearly these two works are on an equal footing in Wagner's admiration, and it is not difficult to discover, in the shrewd and involved prose of the composer of *Tristan*, many a phrase inspired by a common profound passion for the two great pioneers of the symphony.

. . . . .

[69] Richard Wagner, *On a German School of Music*, Tr. Dannreuther.
[70] Ibid., *The Art of Conducting*.
[71] *Ibid.*

SYMPHONY IN G MINOR
Completed 25th July 1788

The scoring was originally, besides strings ('cellos and basses), one flute, two oboes, two bassoons and two horns. Later Mozart replaced the two oboes by two clarinets, while two oboes were added with modified parts. There are no trumpets or drums. The sharp tang of the original oboes must have tended to heighten the true character of the work.

*81—K.550.

With no introduction or preparation at all the composer plunges right into his subject, hasty and uneasy. The theme is stated by the violins, alone, and is accompanied by *divisi* violas. On the second statement the woodwind add some sustained chords; and the sequel to the first subject—really a second subject already, in B flat—reaches the *forte* level. It is impossible to imagine a clearer demarcation between the constituent subjects of the movement: the true second subject, indisputably 'Mozartian' in its chromaticisms, is in fact stated, by strings alone, only after a complete bar's rest:

*82

the response is on oboes and clarinets,[72] and on the second subject being repeated the scoring is interchanged; this time it is stated by the woodwind, strings replying. Then a modu-

[72] Clarinets and bassoons in 'Philharmonia' miniature score. (Tr.)

lating *ritornello* of energetic character opening, *piano*, in A flat, brings us again to the rhythm of the first subject, in a *Coda*, which is twice repeated, to conclude, after a brilliant *ritornello* in unison, in B flat. A single chord before the double bar brings the first part to an abrupt close.

The same slashing chord is again twice repeated, by the whole orchestra, to open the development section. With an abrupt stroke of genius these two chords have served to lead us into the key furthest removed from that of the movement (F sharp minor): the principal theme accordingly appears in this key, with sustained chords on the woodwind:

*83

After modulations and extensions it reappears in the basses, under a new and very energetic figure on the violins; then, in a forceful and magnificent expansion, the basses and violins alternate, bandying the principal subject and the quaver figure in a vigorous development:

*84

The woodwind have sustained chords and the bassoon doubles the bass. The principal subject persists in the violins, while the woodwind present a modified version in counterpoint with it. Very soon the latter respond with the first two quavers of the theme only. A dialogue follows, with this fragment of the initial theme tossed back and forth in contrary motion and with a feverish haste between the basses and the violins. Then the woodwind, unattended, embark on the transition passage designed to lead up to the recapitulation, a phrase whose descending chromaticisms give rise to poignantly expressive modulations:

*85

It will be seen that the development is strictly thematic. The recapitulation is at first identical; but what we have called the sequel to the first subject now gives rise to what is a veritable second development in counterpoint between the first violins and the basses, with the second violins continuing the quaver figure. This sequel to the first subject then reappears, victorious, in the principal key. The same bar's silence, as in the first part, divides the second subject from the foregoing; it is now in the tonic, giving it much more intensity of expression; the layout is the same as on its first appearance, but its continuation undergoes an expressive extension. A *Coda* (not separated by double bars, and based entirely on the opening bars of the theme) sums up energetically and concentrates in a few bars all the expression of this first movement:

*86

an expression which in the last pages takes on a wild and excited character only to sink back finally into a feeling of resigned lassitude.

*87

This is to some extent but an outline, opening in counterpoint with the basses and employing at first only the string quartet; on its repetition a counter-melody soars above in the violins. The austere bareness of this opening, which is to serve as a basis for a song of unsuspected beauty, is immediately suggestive of Bach. From the first violins the second half of this first subject is transferred to the bass, and out of this continuation springs a rising *motif* of two demi-semiquavers, which will permeate the entire movement. It is first woven around the melodic phrase that closes this double exposition of the principal subject in the tonic, now ascending, now descending. It is impossible to overestimate the importance of the basses in all this *Andante*, an importance which Mozart will stress perhaps still more in the *Andante* of the next symphony: we have here as it were a presentiment of what is to come later.

The second subject, separated as in the first movement, is attacked *forte*, in B flat, while its response, constructed out of the aforementioned figure, is heard on the flute and the oboes[73] and concludes in F major. The main theme of the movement then reappears, in D flat, still in counterpoint on the strings, and occasions some bold modulations, while above its implacable solidity the airy demi-semiquavers, now in a descending figure, drop like pearls from the woodwind, glistening and shimmering over these dark depths: the whole clears at

[73] Clarinets in 'Philharmonia' miniature score. (Tr.)

last, leading to a cadence, *forte*, in the dominant.[74] A naïve and unexpected response, forming a third subject, emerges in the strings, as a *Coda*:

*88

it is soon followed by modulations as bold as the preceding ones, making the *ritornello* that concludes the first part, and in which both strings and wind are employed, even more thoroughly 'Mozartian' and angelic.

The development has few equals in expressive depth, even in the works of Mozart. It opens with the rhythm of the principal subject on a unison C flat. To this persistently grave and heavy rhythm is joined the little demi-semiquaver figure, that, as we have already said, pervades all the *Andante*, now cascading from the wind instruments, now gliding from the strings; before finally arriving at the dominant of C minor it runs through the most varied keys; and the return of the principal subject, in C minor, on the woodwind, is first effected by a descending chromatic scale. Over this first subject is now erected a new chromatic figure of an elegaic character, quite 'Wagnerian' and ultra-expressive:

*89

[74] Robert Schumann has remarked that the repeat of the theme in D flat, exactly similar, arises from an error: four bars ought to be omitted in both the first and second parts; and this is confirmed by an examination of the original autograph. These bars are, in the first part, bars 29 to 32, and in the second, bars 48 to 51. See Robert Schumann, *Gesammelte Schriften*, ii, p. 32.

It is so modern and poignant in character, in its brevity, that its *rôle* could not be restricted to that of a simple transition destined to lead back to the recapitulation; Mozart felt it so strongly that he used it again in this recapitulation in a guise perhaps even more expressive:

*90

Notice, too, that it is merely a transposition of the second bar of the initial theme. From the recapitulation of the first subject in G flat the continuation of the astonishing procession is reproduced before our eyes with hardly any changes save those occasioned by its transposition into the main key of the movement.

*91

In spite of the heading *Allegretto* the character of the whole of the minuet is suggestive of a bitter and merciless struggle. The rugged counterpoint of the old masters becomes here the most efficient vehicle of as it were a paroxysm of nervous tension. Twice during the second half the counterpoint is renewed: the minuet theme attacked by the basses after the double bar descends by steps of a third, after which the trebles drag it violently towards the heights; then, following the energetic cadence chords, we have the first bars of the theme, transfigured, given out *piano* by the woodwind alone, they being perhaps better designed to set off the unique moment of sunshine that is the trio (in the major):

*92

Calm, reposeful, pellucid, truly idyllic! The charming curves of the theme are outlined by strings alone, with the response on the woodwind; and in all the second part of this trio the alternation of strings and wind enact an episode so pure and calm, of so Elysian a grace, that in a few bars the tragic adventure of the whole symphony has been obliterated from our minds. Here, exactly as in the first minuet, Mozart, with the sole idea of creating a bond of profound unity between the two, leaves the wind with a short solo passage a few bars before the end.

*93

The *Allegro assai* opens, with an impetuous and demoniac speed, with a theme which, with its refrain:

*94

extends for 32 bars; its double exposition is ensured by repeat marks. The refrain is followed by a long theme in quavers stated first by the violins, then in imitations between the violins and the basses. The impression gained is of a constant opposition between *soli* and *tutti*. Exactly as in the first movement, to which the finale offers some striking similarities, the second subject is clearly separated from the first:

*95

The exposition is entrusted to strings alone, *piano*, and is then passed to the woodwind, varied (melodically and harmonically), and broadened; there is a return to the violin *ritornello* in company with imitations of the opening. As we have again a movement in Sonata Form, this section ends conclusively with big chords in B flat, followed by a double barline.

The development is perhaps of all his work the one wherein Mozart shows the highest degree of passion and even fury. All the resources of his art, rhythm, harmony, counterpoint, are carried to extremes; a contorted, demoniac force has seized him, nor is the listener granted any respite. It is an unusual crisis made manifest by a stroke of genius. Such boldnesses indicate a paroxysm of exaltation, and not free artistic creation. There is no more liberty here, but a mad constraint that seems to leave the composer with not an atom of air to breathe . . . And despite the severity of such a paroxysm—and this is really the core of the Mozartian miracle—neither the characteristic beauty of the work nor its proportions suffer the least injury, nor is the course of the ideas harmed by such violent and cruel shocks.

With Mozart's customary abruptness in a like case, this development opens with the first subject attacked in the key of B flat minor:

*96

then, after a few notes interspersed with rests, the theme is attacked anew, on the dominants of D minor, G minor, C minor and F minor. Canonic imitations appear, first on the flute, then on the bassoon; and now we see a grand *fugato* breaking out among the strings.

One cannot too strongly call attention to this page, in which all the contrapuntal force and the prodigious impetus of which the theme shows itself capable are concentrated.

From the point of view of rhythm and harmony, also from the richness and unexpected variety of its modulations, it seems no exaggeration to say that this *fugato* is one of the monuments of all music; the way the general mood of the movement—of fury and almost delirious exaltation—is strengthened and fortified by its audacious freedom seems to us a transmutation of the technique of the older music to the most 'modern' ends. After a page of combat the imitations, instead of being confined to strings, are exchanged between the woodwind and basses. Both woodwind and basses have a *rôle* of capital importance difficult to over-estimate. It is they alone, the wind, who, after the few bars intercalated with rests with which this quasi-volcanic development opens, unlock the floodgates releasing this musical torrent. So we may say, as the struggle is intensified, so the clashes between wind and basses are exercised in the sharper keys, those furthest removed from the key of the movement, while imperious and sombre horn-calls re-echo.[75]

This persists for two whole pages of the score, with insistent repetitions and a growing boldness, until the struggle is terminated at last on a chord of the diminished seventh.

The recapitulation is at first exact, save for the omission of the second exposition of the principal subject; but the second subject, though not lengthened, is varied. More, its expressive intensity is multiplied tenfold by being cast in G minor, a tonality that for Mozart always bore a marked significance of passionate feverishness. The conclusion also is similar; but by the word conclusion we understand the very last bars, for the final *ritornello* is extended by several bars that moreover contain no hint of appeasement or resignation. An almost furious trans-

[75] It is a bit difficult to follow M. Saint-Foix here, since the horns are silent during the whole of this passage (Tr.)

port of rage persists, with no relenting; we can say that here Mozart exhausts the musical possibilities of such a feeling, and that too without departing from the principal subject on which, in fact, the whole of the development had been based.

While the first movement offered some respite and, towards the end, a sort of resigned lassitude, there is no place here for such lulls; a raging torrent burst its banks, uprooting trees and upheaving boulders. Only the second subject, which with its chromaticisms is but a heartrending plaint when it reappears just before the end, succeeds in interrupting the storm for a few bars only, after which the flood's fury is redoubled and finally sweeps all before it.

. . . . .

The G minor symphony, as we have said already, is the symphony that has occasioned the most characteristic and the greatest number of commentaries. With such a work one is almost justified in saying that these commentaries constitute interpretations. Also we feel bound to quote some of them, with their exact dates, so that the reader can at least estimate the changes wrought by the passage of time when the interpretation of a work of art is in question. The evolution of criticism through the ages seems to us one of the studies most worthy of the attention of the historian.

We know that the Chevalier de Nissen, the second husband of Mozart's widow, busied himself conscientiously in collecting material for a life of Mozart: he has left us, not a life, but only the material for one. The following passage is extracted from this (1828):

'We notice the G minor symphony which offers in its four movements the expression of a restless and uneasy passion, a struggle, a contest with a forcefully penetrating agitation; we notice the E flat symphony, wherein the language is calmer, wherein is no subject for tears; no inconsolable grief, but rather a passion illumined by many a ray of heavenly hope.'[76]

During the same year, 1828, Fétis, in his new *Revue*

[76] Nissen, *Biographie de Mozart*, p. 159.

Musicale (May 11th), sums up his impressions of the G minor symphony, which had been performed at one of the Duchess de Berry's concerts:

'Although Mozart in this symphony has not been lavish in his orchestral demands, although those mass effects that astonish and transport us in the Beethoven symphonies will not be found here, the inventive fire burning in this work, the passionate and energetic tones there poured out, the melancholy hue which prevails, make of it one of the very finest productions of the human mind.'

Later, in writing his article on Mozart in his *Biographie des Musiciens*, he does not hesitate to declare the G minor symphony as 'the discovery of a new world of music'.[77]

If now we turn to the criticism of 'young France' we find ourselves in a noticeably different atmosphere. What Hector Berlioz finds most striking in such a work as the G minor is first of all the grace, delicacy and charm of the melodies, the detail of the workmanship; there is no question of melancholy, still less of passion. There is little between this mode of appreciation and Robert Schumann's, who apropos of this symphony invokes Apollo and the impassive beauty of the Greek temple. But let us follow Berlioz through his years as critic of *La Gazette Musicale*.

6th March 1836: 'Mozart's symphony in G minor, that model of delicacy and naïveté, rendered this time exactly in the style best suited to it, conquered even the most exclusive admirers of Beethoven; the minuet had to be repeated. It would be hard, in truth, to hear anything more charming in grace and loveliness than the *trio* of this movement; and even were it deprived of the spell of such perfect playing it would, I believe, never fail in its effect.'

9th April 1840: 'G minor symphony, Mozart. First movement admirably fashioned and full of charming fancies; *Adagio* tender, quiet, calm and delicate; the minuet, vigorous opening, deliciously graceful and naïve in the middle; the finale, full of verve, strewn with fragments of adorable melody.'

[77] Fétis: 6, p. 243.

Finally, 28th February 1841: 'Mozart's G minor symphony opened the proceedings; it is very melodious, very distinguished, very delicately wrought; the *trio* of the minuet is a masterpiece of naïve grace which could scarcely be surpassed. I say the *trio*, for the minuet itself ranks for me among the sort of broad jokes I spoke of the other day in connection with Haydn.'

We have here a very widespread opinion among the average audience, and a most persistent one. Fifty years later it will have changed scarcely at all. We see that listening to a symphony has become a serious matter; Haydn laughed too much, or tried to make us laugh too often; in 1840 simple and joyous high spirits were hardly admissible when 'learned' music was in question. But it must be understood that if the majority of eighteenth century minuets—and several types are distinguishable—are put in 'the category of jokes', it is really impossible to commit a greater error than to include the minuet of the G minor symphony. In fact, of the whole classical epoch it is the one minuet whose inspiration springs from the same source as the more scientifically constructed movements of the symphony.

The new and audacious criticism by the romantics, interesting and strong when dealing with contemporary work, was just as ordinary or most often content with commonplaces as soon as the work of the preceding generation came to the surface. Their ideals, no doubt very high, precluded all understanding of the farcical, sometimes 'smart', art with which the eighteenth century was crammed. It was agreed among the 'highbrow' amateurs that Boccherini was no longer bearable; Berlioz emphasizes the *'gaudrioles'* of Haydn; Mozart is pardoned with some difficulty for a few bars of instrumental figuration entrusted to Donna Anna, meditating in her Chapel, at the end of *Don Giovanni*. This seems to arise from two distinct causes. Art, generally speaking, tends towards a more severe and grander end; it becomes more individualistic and does not shrink from serving as a constant expression of the personal feelings of the artist, even the most intimate; on the other hand, ignorance of the past, even the near past, clouds everything with so thick a veil that no one can hope to lift it. All the enormous richness of musical Italy, vocal and instrumental, remains a dead letter.

But there was at that time, in the heart of the steppes of Central Russia, a man whose ardent love of Mozart's work evoked so profound, living and a clear vision of this work, that he may well be considered the first of the master's real biographers. To his gift of subtle insight were added natural and imaginative qualities of style which allowed him to describe with all the brilliance and fire of his temperament, any of Mozart's works, whether operatic, instrumental or sacred. No one before him had even attempted to span so considerable and diverse a work. Moreover, no book quite like this had ever been devoted to a musician! It is not that of a pedagogue, still less that of an amateur; the analyses it provides of the great creations of Mozart's genius are almost always really poetical transformations, but they are backed by a sufficiently informed musical knowledge to give them value and solidity. We have already here an example of sound and trustworthy musicology, and we long to quote whole pages. But we must limit ourselves. We shall draw attention to some striking passages dealing with the G minor symphony which will give the reader some idea of a work that is, in our opinion, without precedent, for until that time no one had had the least idea of a 'musical biography'.

It was therefore to a Russian nobleman, Alexander Dimitrievich Oulibicheff (1791-1858), that fell the honour of having attempted the first 'musical' biographical study of Mozart.[78] In analysing his principal works in chronological order he has in fact written something very like a 'musical life' of the master; the host of needless digressions, it will be realised, is evidence of the leisure the noble dilettante enjoyed, and it will be understood that all the part treating of musical history and, in general, his writings on Beethoven's aesthetic are nowadays entirely in disrepute. But I do not know of the existence, even today, of many analyses of Mozart's dramatic works that are comparable

[78] *Nouvelle Biographie de Mozart* followed by a sketch of the general history of music and *l'Analyse des Principales Œuvres de Mozart* (3 volumes), Moscow, Semen, 1843.

with his, as much from the truly psychological as the musical point of view; furthermore, no one before him had written so extensively or brought to bear so much imagination in commenting on a single quartet or symphony. It would even be desirable, both out of respect to this direct ancestor of the science of musicology, and out of admiration for his amazing 'Mozartian' insight, to consider a re-issue of his work limiting oneself, however, to the third volume. The author's Slav mysticism enables him to enter the most secret places of the heart, and to translate into words something that does really give a little idea of the mysterious beauty of the *Andante* of the G minor symphony:

'. . . But what vision glimpsed through the ivory gates of Elysium, or rather what distant, dim hope has come to stay this grief, to solace the soul like some divine balm applied to its wounds? *Andante* 6/8 E flat major, one of those unfathomable works wherein all is revelation for the feelings and mystery for the mind. The theme is somewhat vague in its contours, complex in form, and it is *precisely* from this fact that the movement draws the magic of its effect, and an angelic expression that attains the supernatural. A close inspection is required to convince oneself that this masterpiece, varied and rich in figuration as it appears, is built entirely on the first four bars, with in addition another idea, inseparable from the theme but of quite a different aspect. This is a little figure of demi-semi-quavers, grouped in pairs, whose fluttering of wings is heard mingling with the weightiest syncopations, the most picturesque harmonic progressions, the most unexpected flights of modulation, the most abstruse thematic "analysis". Add to this a limpid and as it were prismatic scoring, the same details coloured with a multitude of different tints according as they are entrusted to the bow or human lips; and amidst this harmonious ferment float fragments of song straight from heaven, as a breath of scent-laden air.'[79]

And later, dealing with the transport of passion evident in the finale:

[79] *Nouvelle Biographie de Mozart*, vol. iii, p. 257.

'I doubt if there exists in all music anything more deeply incisive, more cruelly anguished, more violently distracted, more agonisingly passionate than the second half of this finale. And in achieving so exuberant an expression Mozart has employed hardly any means but the main theme, whose *motif*, at first founded on the intervals of the triad, here utilises the intervals of the minor ninth and other harmonic acerbities. The theme, too, here splits up in canonic form between the two phalanxes of the orchestra, battling against hostile countersubjects in its furious march, and soon hurled to the ground; then, victor in its turn, you hear it driving pitilessly and relentlessly in a succession of chords which, sharper and sharper, push it to the furthest remove from its primitive tonality; and all this continues for 80 bars. From what incident of his inner life, what paroxysm of the heart, has Mozart drawn this frenzied yet classic inspiration! How has this abundance of passion sprung from such an abundance of skill!'[80] The Russian critic, in the lines following, sums up the general impression made on him by the G minor symphony; his refined appreciation, in fact, corroborates that of the first hearers of the masterpiece:

'The G minor symphony, like the quintet in the same key, expresses the disturbance of passion, the longing and regret of an unhappy love, but it expresses them with the difference that here we have a plaint concentrated, in the depths of his own soul, or at most suffered vicariously through the sympathy of a friend, on a grief without reserve and without bounds, bursting in the face of the whole world, which it would fill with its lamentations.'[81]

On almost every page of the book similar appraisals are to be found; Berlioz apart, music had never, we believe, been previously spoken of in like terms. The Russian critic wrote these lines about the year 1841: who knows? perhaps we see in him the Sainte-Beuve of musical criticism, with his enthusiasms and his prejudices; in any case, we see in him a man not content

[80] *Nouvelle Biographie de Mozart*, p. 259-260.
[81] *Ibid.*, p. 255.

Musikalischer Spaß

für

Violinen, Bratsche, zwei Hörner u. Baß

geschrieben in Wien den 14ten Juny 1787

von

W. A. MOZART!

93tes Werk.

nach dem Originalmanuscripte des Autors herausgegeben

No 1508.   Preis f 2.

Offenbach a/m, bei J. André.

with anecdotes more or less diverting, but one who speaks of music with the finest discrimination, one who goes to the root of the matter and boldly plunges into the realm of psychology. He is at home there with the easy elegance of the diplomat who has learned to know his fellow men; in artistic matters he gives judgment with a clear vision free from all pedantry. But for any musical work dating after about 1815 or 1820 one feels that his sensitivity is dulled and his judgment warped. For bear in mind that he was born in 1791, the very year of Mozart's death! Who then of his generation would have grasped the significance of Beethoven's last works, or of the first flowerings of romanticism? On the other hand, those who did feel the transcendance of the work of the later Beethoven relegated all Mozart's instrumental work, *ipso facto*, to the second class. The main point is that no one had as yet (that is, before 1841), surveyed this work with so acute and comprehensive a glance.

Unhappily, the book was not able to exorcise a sort of decline, or at least a slackening off in the interest aroused by Mozart's instrumental music in the second half of the nineteenth century. In contrast to this his dramatic works continued to have a following, and at every production of one or other of his operas their success had been maintained, or even heightened. And that up till the moment when, the Wagnerian movement absorbing everything, Mozart's vocal and symphonic work had disappeared almost completely below the horizon. 'Wagnerism' admitted scarcely anything but the Beethoven of the last quartets, the Mass in D and the Choral Symphony.

And here we must note the most curious phenomenon of all. For, if we have established the almost complete disappearance of Mozart's symphonic works from the programmes of the great concerts of the Wagner period, and even if a certain disdain for his work in general is in evidence at this time, it is all the more surprising to learn that the most undoubtedly illustrious of all the Wagnerians—Richard Wagner himself—has revealed himself as the most ardent and comprehensive protagonist of Mozart's three great symphonies. The perusal of Volume IX of his writings came as a surprise and a revelation to us. What we have said above of his preoccupations relative to the interpretation of Mozart, and especially of the E flat symphony, of which he demonstrates the artistic sense and importance equally with regard to the first movement and the finale, has already thrown a sufficient light on his 'Mozartian' feeling.[82]

When he had the opportunity of hearing the G minor symphony at the famous concerts at the Odeon (Conservatoire) in Munich, the detailed description of the *Andante* (from which he quotes three passages) and the ironic criticism he gives of this performance enable one to see the extent of his admiration, and how much he felt the interpretation of a great masterpiece (victim of an already long-standing tradition) left to be desired. The passage should be quoted in its entirety.

'. . . I was present at the performance of the G minor symphony of Mozart. The manner in which the *Andante* of the symphony was played, and the effect it produced was altogether inconceivable. Who has not, in his youth, admired this beautiful piece, and tried to realise it in his own way? In what way? No matter. If the marks of expression are scanty, the wonderful composition arouses one's feelings; and fancy supplies the means to read it in accordance with such feelings. It seems as if Mozart had expected something of the kind, for he has given but few and meagre indications of the expressions. So we felt free to indulge ourselves in the delicately increasing swing of the quavers, with the moon-like rise of the violins; the notes of which we believed to sound softly legato:

*98

the tenderly whispering:

*99

[82] Wagner, *op. cit.*

touched us as with wings of angels, and before the solemn
admonitions and questionings of:

*100

(which, however, we heard in a finely sustained *crescendo*) we
imagined ourselves led to a blissful evanescence, which came
upon us with the final bars. Fancies of this sort, however, were
not permitted during the strictly classical performance under
the veteran Kapellmeister, at the Munich Odeon: the proceedings, there, were carried on with a degree of solemnity enough
to make one's flesh creep with a sensation akin to a foretaste of
eternal perdition.

'The lightly floating *Andante* was converted into a ponderous
Largo; not the hundredth part of the weight of a single quaver
was spared us; stiff and ghastly, like a bronze pigtail, the *battuta*
of the *Andante* was swung over our heads; even the feathers of
the angels' wings were turned into corkscrew curls—rigid, like
those of the Seven Years' War. Already, I felt myself placed
under the staff of a Prussian recruiting officer, A.D. 1740, and
longed to be bought off—but! who can guess my terror, when
the veteran turned back the pages, and recommenced his
Largo-Andante merely to do 'Classical' justice to the two little
dots before the double bar in the score! I looked about me for
help and succour—and beheld another wondrous thing: the
audience listened patiently, quite convinced that everything
was in the best possible order, and that they were having a
true Mozartian "feast for the ears" in all innocence and safety.
This being so, I acquiesced and bowed my head in silence.'[83]

Certainly, nothing comparable has been written on Mozart
since Oulibicheff. No commentary by his accredited biographers has this ring: we cannot be too astonished for our own
part, for we had been struck, Wyzewa first, by evident quasi-

[83] Richard Wagner, *On Conducting* (Dannreuther's translation, p. 62
et seq.)

Wagnerian kinship spread over different periods of Mozart's career. But we would not have dared to point them out in so pungent a fashion; under the pretext of teaching the art of conducting, or simply proffering advice, Wagner unveils all his sensitivity and understanding in the presence of master-pieces usually considered as the furthest removed from his own art and thought. Besides, his insistence on the degree of error and incomprehension that prevails over the question of the inter-pretation of Mozart's instrumental works shows how profound was his response and what artistic value he attributes to them. It was in great measure for the maintenance of their cult and the revival of their spirit that he solicited from his sovereign the favour of being allowed to create a new School of Music in Germany. But he always put Mozart's vocal or theatrical work first, and it is probable that of the instrumental music he knew only the last three symphonies. However that may be, these occupy a prominent place in his thoughts and artistic preoccupations.

Today, it can be stated without exaggeration that in publish-ing the fifth edition of Otto Jahn's celebrated Life of Mozart, Herr Hermann Abert has almost supplanted the work of his predecessor.[84] His work constitutes one of the finest monu-ments erected to the glory of Mozart's genius: he illumines all its aspects without forcing all Mozart's output, willy-nilly, into the framework of a pre-established aesthetic; we feel so much, on reading Herr Abert's two volumes, what was the universality of Mozart's genius that this demonstration becomes a veritable revelation. It can be said of these two volumes that they complete the overthrow of nearly all that the criticism of the romantic period would admit on the subject of Mozart, not merely as to the theatrical work, but equally concerning the instrumental output and the sacred music. It is a Mozart completely stripped of the costume in which Otto Jahn had clothed him according to the fashions of the 1860's. From now on this fifth edition is an entirely new book with little

[84] Hermann Abert, *W. A. Mozart* (2 vols.) Leipzig, Breitkopf and Härtel (1921).

connection with the work of its precursor; everything in the latter that was merely conventional has become transformed into significance. For our part, the author has opened up horizons so new and vast that we can still hardly visualise the goal further research will attain. Those who believe the subject of Mozart to be exhausted are given the lie by Herr Abert's two volumes. Equally in the field of human psychology[85] as in that of aesthetic and documentary study, these two volumes of German musicology are an inducement to delve into everything, even what is apparently frivolous.

The analysis of the great symphonies proves to what a slender degree of understanding we were until then accustomed with regard to these masterpieces—with the exception, we must add immediately, of those veritable and penetrating aesthetical and musicological analyses of Alexander Oulibicheff, and Richard Wagner's confessions. For the first time Herr Abert shows us the direct kinship between the great introduction to the E flat symphony and the dramatic preface to *Don Giovanni*; in stressing the already profoundly romantic character of this symphony he thus prepares us for the description of another drama, quite as forceful though more concise, which is none other than the G minor symphony: the analytical pictures he draws of this, and of Mozart's symphonic apotheosis (the C major symphony, the 'Jupiter') are real interpretations, out of which the author derives a new philosophy which he elucidates with a rare felicity of expression. From the examination of the texts springs at once their 'intellectual' interpretation, and we thus see revealed what is still almost unsuspected, namely, the profound meaning of the orchestral masterpiece. Here is surely the most profound commentary to which the instrumental work of Mozart in its final stages has given rise.

We had already established that Mozart's last three symphonies, nearly contemporaneous with *Don Giovanni*, marked the apex of his romantic career: reading the various commentaries inspired by one or other of them affords some confirm-

[85] See particularly the remarkable chapter entitled: *Mozart's Personality*, ii, p. 1.

ation of this fact. What has been written with pen of flame would naturally excite the most glowing and ardent description; and nowhere are there to be found any appreciations comparable with those that *Don Giovanni* and the G minor symphony have inspired. For the latter, we have been able to follow the *crescendo* of admiration extended to it by critics since its first performances in France and Germany, until the time of the publications of Oulibicheff (1843), Otto Jahn (1856), Richard Wagner (1865-69), and Herr Abert (1921). Between these two last works criticism recognised with great difficulty the passionate character of the symphony; it insisted, as indeed for every work dating from the eighteenth century, on its graceful movement, or simply on its melancholy. For us the G minor symphony, with a more reduced orchestra than in Mozart's other great symphonic compositions, translates the inner unrest of a mind that has always chosen this key for the expression of feelings of ardent and troubled melancholy, infinitely impassioned.

. . . . .

Symphony in C major (The Jupiter)[86]
Completed 10th August 1788

The orchestra includes, besides the string quartet (where 'cellos are quite distinct from the double basses), one flute, two oboes, two bassoons, two horns (in C), two trumpets (in C), and timpani (C,G).

*101—K.551.

The first part of the movement (before the double barline), can be divided into five sections, separated from each other

---

[86] The person responsible for this nickname, dating certainly from after the death of Mozart, is unknown.

sometimes by a pedal point, or by pauses twice lasting three beats of a bar, and once, to make the contrast even more marked, by a whole bar. From these five portions we get an impression of vital force that often enhances the martial, heroic character which the movement owes to the march rhythm of the wind instruments.

The work opens with a rough triplet figure, a sort of 'appel heroique' to be found in many a symphony or overture, here intensified by the unison of strings and wind. This principle of masculine affirmation is at once succeeded by a sort of plaintive questioning, clearly standing for the expressive, feminine principle, as distinct from the dominating element stated at the beginning of the movement. Then, a new opposition between this dominating force stated once more, now in the dominant, and the same response, a degree higher and thus rendered even more expressive. The latter is quickly cut short by an orchestral *tutti*, with the whole of the wind outlining a solemn but lively march, punctuated by big chords on the first violins. Between these emphatic chords the second violins and violas are heard with a descending flourish seemingly corresponding to the rising triplets of the opening. All this constitutes a *ritornello* of great dignity, proclaiming a sort of triumph closely akin to that Mozart will later write to open his *Clemenza di Tito*. What we have called the first section, the foundation stone of the building, closes with a long pedal point ending with the whole orchestra in unison, on the dominant. So behold this corner stone, laid before us with the most irresistible vigour and clearness, in the full, frank light of C major.

But now a tiny cloud appears in the sky. The opening theme is repeated, but *piano*, as it were softened and overcome by a new figure (flute and oboe), which modifies and refines its first roughness; the response, which seemed just now restrained and almost stifled, is extended:

*102

135

diversified by the dramatic inflexions so peculiar to Mozart, and is to play an essential *rôle* in this second section of the movement. In fact, from the moment when the first bar of Ex.101 has re-echoed, *forte*, in the dominant, this melodic response becomes so warm and intense that its rhythm dominates the orchestra and its importance becomes preponderating in all the rest of the movement; but despite its melodic character and ardent expression, the horns and trumpets maintain the march rhythm, accentuated, and reproduce in a slightly abridged form the martial *ritornello* that formerly ended on the dominant, over a pedal point, and which is here brusquely interrupted by a chord of the dominant of G. After three beats' rest the true second subject of the movement emerges in the first violins:

*103

to which the basses will later reply with a sort of evocative echo of the above-mentioned melodic response (bar 71); in the second exposition of this subject the first violins are joined by the bassoon, and later by the flute, without in the least detracting from its airy suppleness. Its length is such that by itself it fills the whole of this third section; and that shows to what extent Mozart delighted in dialogues between the members of the quartet during this episode, which exceeds in length all the second subjects of his symphonies.

But the heroic atmosphere of the symphony cannot allow this second subject to be established too firmly, as its delightful suppleness runs the risk of modifying the general character of the movement. So everything is cut short abruptly; there is a whole bar's rest, then the outburst, *forte*, in the minor:

leading very quickly to a *ritornello* demonstrating anew the force of that melodic response which simultaneously plays a *rôle* both expressive and rhythmic, a *rôle* whose importance in the movement is certainly as great as that of the separate subjects constituting it. In it, in fact, there lies an intrinsic power that spreads throughout the whole movement, with the exception, however, of the development.

Then, after a new bar on an unexpected figure on the dominant of G major, a new figure emerges in this key, light in character, straight out of *opera buffa*:[87]

*105

Seeing this bubbling up in its carefree buoyancy, one would never guess that from it, or more exactly from its immediate sequence, would spring all the first part of that enormous development, one of Mozart's most spacious and powerful! This fifth section of the movement demonstrates its unwonted breadth; it surpasses the usual limits of the master's great symphonies, and brings to the general gravity of the work a playful note from which Mozart can draw more science than from a theme more inherently 'scholastic'. Finally, the first part of the movement concludes with a *ritornello* in which, at

[87] It had appeared already in an air written by Mozart in May 1788, for Albertarelli, to the words: *Voi siete un po tondo, mio caro Pompeo, l'usanze del mondo andate a studdiar.*

the very end, the figure or roulade in descending demi-semi-quavers that has already intruded in the first two sections of the movement takes a prominent part.

The development opens with two bars of flutes, oboes and bassoons in unison, taking us quietly and almost playfully into the dark key of E flat major. With the same bass accompaniment and the same viola *pizzicato*, but this time in E flat, we are re-introduced to the charming and unexpected theme that had served as a conclusion to the first part (Ex. 105). It is a curious thing, as we have already remarked, that the most scholarly part of the work has been drawn from this theme, or rather, from its last bar, which is at once repeated by oboes and bassoons accompanied by the basses *pizz*. This bar is immediately interchanged between violins and basses while the march rhythm that we have noticed earlier reappears in the wind; after six bars the counterpoint becomes more closely knit, the two groups are thrown against each other in the same bar, beneath sustained chords on the wind, until the basses seize the subject and exhaust its 'potential'; they conduct it to the point where it serves only as a transition leading back to the first subject, after two bars of unaccompanied woodwind have brought us to rest on the dominant of A minor:

*106

All this is but a dry analysis; but how can one give any idea whatever of the vitality that emerges, the most symphonically in the world, from all this development? Never has the term *development* been used in a more correct and inspired sense than here: while the woodwind are outlining lofty and joyous rhythms, while the strings exchange among themselves that little figure derived from the simple final cadence of the third and last subject of the movement, and while all this is combined by an intrinsic force capable of unifying all and still ruling, behold the miracle by which Mozart, at grips with the most diverse elements of symphony, chamber music or operatic finale, becomes the supreme master sporting divinely with these elements.

But the development is not finished, and as it were a second one now commences: for the size of this last symphony is going to surpass all expectation! Nearly seven pages of the Eulenburg miniature score are filled by the development of the first movement, which has a total length of twenty-nine pages. So after a few bars, wherein we see the final expiry of the little figure that has been the mainspring of all the development so far, in passing from the dominant of A minor to the key of F major, we shall witness a new and powerful development, opening with a return to the principal subject in F—a circumstance at once directing our minds to a procedure especially dear to Joseph Haydn and which has been designated by the term False Recapitulation. We have here, indeed, just such a false recapitulation; this sly and unexpected return of the principal theme, *piano*, in improvisatory fashion, and at first seemingly intent on passing unperceived, becomes firmly established in the orchestra; each repetition takes it a degree higher in the scale, with constant support from the chromaticisms of the woodwind; on its first appearance, in F, it is still followed by its melodic response, but from the second appearance onwards this has vanished. Events move rapidly, and the conflict threatens. It breaks out on a chord of A minor; then, over a bass descending semitone by semitone, with syncopated chords in the woodwind, a violent struggle flares up between the triplet figure with which the movement began, and that launched by the second violins and violas under the martial calls of the wind. These two contrary figures, the one ascending, the other descending, are given at first to the violins, who hurl and hustle them through the roughest tonalities, until the basses seize on the second and bring it to a halt on the dominant. Next, the cadence of the third subject from which all the first development had sprung reappears in the first violins, and in the space of eight bars leads to the recapitulation. But this cadence, so fertile in unforeseen counterpoints, is again to give rise in this space to a masterly stroke, allotted to the woodwind alone; and it is an unalloyed pleasure to see, or hear, the oboes and bassoons yielding to new ideas, such as the great working-out of this unique figure in the first development had not allowed us to foresee. Such is the magnificent scaffolding: when at first the master magician showed us the two or three poor little fragments that were to be used in constructing it and raising it up in all its grandeur we certainly could not have deduced the technical and aesthetic result obtained by Mozart—a power uniquely musical wherein genius itself is forgotten.

In the great works of Mozart the repercussion exercised by similar developments on the subsequent course of the movement is so considerable that, even where the recapitulation is identical with the opening, its component elements are seen to be as it were transfigured: there is an occult and inexpressible force, a sort of surging of the elements stirred by the powerful, all-commanding helm. And that is the impression we get of this recapitulation; the only changes appear in the second statement of the theme after the long pedal point on the dominant. The second statement this time is in the minor, and the melodic response gives rise to some counterpoint that yields an elevated moment of six bars duration.

*107

By their reappearance all the elements of the movement acquire that character of definitive significance that a single exposition could not confer on them, and it is perhaps in this fact that we can find rational justification for the repetition of all the elements of a movement, so often criticised by the non-musical. There remains nothing now but the conclusion. Mozart simply adds a few bars in which resounds a fanfare that winds up the first movement of the 'Jupiter' in a mood of joyous steadfastness.

The theme is stated by the first violins *con sordini*; it is joined in the lower octave by the seconds, then accompanied by them and the violas, both muted. Its length (ten bars) is as remarkable as its expression. It can be looked upon as formed of two phrases; the second, beginning at the seventh bar, is a song of warm and expansive tenderness, so spontaneous that it becomes almost an outburst of this feeling, as if the heart could no longer contain it. The sentence finishes and, having concluded in the tonic, the melody then passes to the violas and basses ('cellos and double basses), with repeated chords on horns and bassoons in support; almost at once the violins reply to this melody with a figure in demi-semiquavers, an offshoot of the theme itself, leading by a beautiful descending curve to the dominant, and the second subject.

The latter by successive stages reaches its culmination at the end of its seventh bar; it begins in the minor, and immediately syncopations and sighs throw us into an atmosphere of trouble and grief, and that, too, most 'modern' in feeling; the chords of the ninth and the audacious modulations combine to create an impression very near to that of many Wagnerian fragments; but with the transience of a cloud melting before the rays of the sun—and, we might add, with something of the same nature— the third subject appears in the first violins accompanied by embroidery in the seconds and with the basses in contrary motion. This is a rising phrase, like the preceding one, floating in a limitless ether; it is answered by a figure in sextolets destined to play an important part in the remainder of this *Andante*, a figure whose varied and charming curves have a melancholy tinge, probably due to the impression left by the second subject. It is necessary to insist on the length of these subjects, particularly the last, which is followed by a *ritornello* in the form of a dialogue between wind and strings; this over, the first violins, still preserving the sextolet motion, help us over the double bar, alone and unaided, in the most original fashion.

This unexpected transition has something of the air of a recitative. But it has gone scarcely four bars before the wind have already repeated the second subject, perhaps even more plaintive than on its first presentation. From D minor we pass to E flat minor, and arrive at the recapitulation by means of a dialogue between wind and strings fashioned out of a fragment of the preceding sextolets, flowing in incessant chromaticisms.

But what changes in this recapitulation! Scarcely has the first bar of the theme sounded in the first violins, than the slurred demi-semiquaver figure that answered the initial theme in the first part of the *Andante* appears in the basses; by its very nature this vast flowing figure so belongs to the violins that they now seize it afresh; it is interrupted, however, to allow the first bar of the theme to resound in the basses, in B flat. Then, *forte*, the torrent of demi-semiquavers sweeps from under the bows, with 'appels heroiques' from the wind: the culminating point is reached in a veritable fracas over the dominant; a *fortissimo* blazes out, with the demi-semiquavers in the basses, the woodwind and horns hammering out their rhythm on the chord of C major and the violins slashing great chords across three strings. Then, with no transition, a brief echo of the second subject is heard, as it were a sob quickly stifled; and the third subject reappears complete with its expressive continuation suffused with an Elysian calm and heightened by new wonders in the treatment of the wind. The dialogue noticed above is reproduced, leading to one of the most beautiful *Codas* Mozart has ever conceived.

The first bar of the theme is sung, as at first, by the first violins; but in place of the second the demi-semiquaver figure appears, *piano*, on the flute and bassoon in octaves. The second half of the theme, so intensely expressive, and which had been omitted in the recapitulation, is here reproduced in its entirety, in all its ravishing simplicity; and of the long figure in sextolets there remains only the last two bars of the movement,

a sort of far off, poetic echo, expiring in a *pianissimo* not unlike
the ending of the slow movement of the G minor symphony.[88]

*109

This minuet is assuredly one of the most original Mozart
ever wrote for symphony orchestra. It should be noted that it
comprises but a single subject and constitutes a perfect little
Sonata Form movement, with development and recapitulation.
The same could be said of other minuets; but this one seems to
form an even more homogeneous whole.

With its chromaticisms, it offers us at the outset a language
whose sensuality is interrupted, nine bars after the double barline, only to allow the wind instruments to ring out, unaccompanied by strings: chromaticisms, symphonic writing of the
richest kind, the use of the wind, all put us in mind of Wagner;
and the likeness becomes even more obvious when a few bars
before the end the wind, entirely unaccompanied, interlace
their chromatically descending lines! This passage for unaccompanied wind does in fact reproduce the procedure Mozart
employs in the corresponding place in the minuet of the G
minor symphony, but how much developed and amplified here!
The outstandingly 'modern' character of this minuet is affirmed
by the intensive use of counterpoint, almost presaging the *rôle*
this will play in the ensuing finale. The *trio*, likewise, seems to
herald the near approach of the famous finale; the first notes of
the latter are, in fact, already outlined in the first violin part,
immediately after the double bar.

This anticipation is worthy of remark, for the first notes of
the succeeding finale must have assumed a definite significance

[88] This fine ending replaces another, shorter one. See Abert, ii., p.
133.

in Mozart's work. They are in fact to be found scattered among several works of different character—mass, symphony, sonata for violin and piano—but it is in the coming finale that they receive their definite and final consecration.

*110

This famous movement, considered, and with justification, perhaps the veritable symphonic testament of Mozart, is not a fugue as has so often been stated. It is a complex ensemble, very difficult to classify in pre-established forms, in which counterpoint plays a preponderant *rôle* destined to reveal Mozart as complete master of his resources. But it is first and foremost a movement in *Sonata Form*, with repeat bars, development and varied recapitulation, followed by a grand *Coda*.

This preponderating use of *fugato* in a symphonic finale was not unprecedented. The Austrian instrumental school has examples to offer that have become known only recently: probably under the influence of the old contrapuntist Fux, whose not inconsiderable reaction is felt up to the time of Beethoven, such masters as Georg Mathias Monn, Dittersdorf, Michael Haydn (a first hand exemplar for Mozart) practised the *fugato* finale form in their symphonies, without, of course, even remotely approaching the effect that Mozart here obtained. What is worthy of note here is the co-existence of the scholastic element in a quartet or symphony finale side by side with other themes of a less severe nature, even popular or trifling; the best example of this *genre* is the finale of the first of the six quartets dedicated to Joseph Haydn. Nevertheless here the quality of the themes does not present such an alloy, and their combination does not offer so striking a contrast: the general bearing of the symphony, which, one feels, Mozart has thoroughly understood, does not allow of such licence in the choice of material. And that the very diverse and individual themes forming the substance of the present finale should cohere into such admirable unity is not the least astonishing merit of this gigantic musical peroration.

It is possible to distinguish three gigantic fragments composing in reality the first portion of the movement. In the first of these the themes (a) and (b) figure; the first actually comprising two halves, one formed of the four note *motif*, familiar since, as we have remarked, it forms a favourite group used by Mozart in many a vocal and instrumental work, while the other plays only a brilliant and homophonic *rôle* and will be used in the *ritornello* and at the end of the *Coda*.

The movement opens with an astonishingly simple melodic phrase, stated by the first violins to an accompaniment of slurred quavers in the seconds. The whole orchestra is at once brought into play for the counter-statement; the melody continues to be entrusted to the violins, but *staccato*, while in the treble the wind is busy with a severe *motif*, in suspensions, and in the bass the lower strings trace roulades of three or four semiquavers, clearly derived from the four semiquavers that give a sort of surge to the refrain. The first subject being now ended in the tonic, a new idea, (b), clear and vigorous, arises. It is easy to see that it will lend itself to numerous combinations; it engenders and demands contrapuntal treatment. But one could scarcely suspect its hidden force of attraction in this regard. Here it is as it is first heard:

*III

Over a bass moving by contrary motion it climbs a third higher, presently to reappear in the wittiest and most unexpected fashion, divested of all its weighty and majestic contrapuntal character, piped by a solo flute as a response to the true *cantabile* subject of the movement, in the third section of the finale (Ex.113). A brilliant *ritornello*, quite homophonic, brings us to rest on the dominant.

The second period opens with the initial semibreves, *piano*, attacked first by the second violins, next by the firsts, then the violas, and lastly by the basses; veritable fugal entries, following each other at intervals of three and four bars. Strictly limited to the string quartet at first, this dominating theme is then repeated in octaves by the upper parts (violins, flutes and oboes), with a new sequel:

*112

giving rise in its turn to imitations between violins and basses, supported by the whole of the wind; and as this section is to be devoted wholly to polyphony, it is not surprising to find *motif* (b) reappearing here, as a *codetta*, generating imitations at half a bar's distance. This contraction does not really allow sufficient time for the imitations to be clearly heard in so quick a movement; we would go so far as to say its character here becomes a trifle flurried.

We now have the *cantabile* subject of the movement:

which opens the third section in G major. Stated *piano* by the first violins to a quaver accompaniment in the seconds, exactly as the first subject, it is succeeded by the witty response derived from theme (b), already noted above (page 146): by its very 'Mozartian' grace, its delicate playfulness, it seems to exclude the severity and roughness of counterpoint. But no such thing: Mozart here is as insistent as possible, and seems bent on demonstrating to future generations the resources of the old language, its richness and persuasive force. We are fully in agreement with Herr Abert, who does not hesitate to recognise in the composer of *Don Giovanni* the last representative of the old school of contrapuntists, those for whom counterpoint was neither an effort nor a display of learning but a mode of expression, a language that Mozart revived, all the resources of which he was able to adapt to the needs of modern thought.

His way of combining this melodious subject with the sequel to the first subject quoted in Ex.112 and *motif* (b) (Ex.111) is as dexterous as it is audacious. It is a dialogue in which counterpoint becomes mocking and carefree. First, flutes and bassoons, in imitation, exchange Ex.112 between them to the accompaniment of a running violin figure; we next behold the subject that had seemed uniquely melodic (Ex.113) transformed into a fugal entry, retaining no more than its first three minims and, shedding its singing character, acquiring an unforeseen vigour and becoming clearly scholastic:

It is interchanged between the first violins and the basses, while the second violins and the violas are themselves engaged in a spirited duel in quavers. But Mozart is about to show us that it is not only the three opening notes of Ex.113 which are capable of becoming very respectable fugal entries, but the entire theme. And now, the battle being first joined by the strings, with the woodwind admitting in the first place only the three minims mentioned above, feeling runs so high that they fling themselves bravely into the *mêlée*; and so powerful is the surge of all this that what we have called the refrain of the initial subject blazes up with a brilliance so vivid that, suddenly, all counterpoint ceases and the homophony of the refrain gains the mastery. But this simple refrain, growing in force and extent, is quickly seized by the basses, modulates, and leads to some brusque imitations of (b) which will later resolve into a *ritornello* destined to close the first part in the key of the dominant. Our description would seem to indicate a cadence, *forte*, in a brilliant style; this astonishing movement yields on the contrary the surprise of ending with a short *Coda* through which flits *motif* (b), first on the oboe and repeated by the bassoon.

After this contest, of which words are powerless to convey its variety and spirit, its verve and dominating energy, what could possibly be the development now about to commence? What development can follow the two developments already completed?

It opens after the double bar with the return of the principal subject, like all regularly constructed Sonata Form movements. It modulates at once to C minor; the wind replies, *piano*, with *motif* (b), on oboe and bassoon; and these three first bars of the second part are sufficient, solely by means of modulation, to throw a mysterious veil over the first subject:

*115

when the latter reappears over the dominant of A minor the same response is introduced anew, but inverted, and the bitter conflict that had previously been unleashed in the course of the second section is at once renewed. Here, at half a bar's distance, imitations between basses, violins and wind are built up once more; we have previously remarked on their compression and speed, *motif* (b) opening with a dotted crotchet followed by a quaver bursting so promptly in the various instrumental groups that their successive discharges have insufficient time to be clearly heard by the listener. We have mentioned how (b) was developed in both ascending and descending fashion; when it occurs in ascending form, giving rise to a like combat in a clash of imitations, Mozart finds means of intercalating the first subject between each new attack, modulating fifth upon fifth, and stated by wind alone. Here is the lay-out, quasi-Tristanesque in style:

*116

The incessant and aggressive response (b) which has become a forceful and leading theme continues in the strings until, on the dominant of E minor and sounding in unison, the master's genius requires six bars only in which to get back to the principal subject in the original key. The passage is worth quoting:

This is a powerful abridgement. The recapitulation will provide another, not less energetic. The principal subject is stated, as at first, by the first violins, accompanied in the same fashion by the slurred quavers in the seconds; but the woodwind join in rather earlier, before the energetic counter-statement, *staccato*, on the violins; the basses again roll out their figure, rising and falling like the waves of the ocean. Not content with the three or four bars of the exposition they here extend through twenty bars, and enter many harmonic domains; their impact has the effect of deepening considerably all this recapitulation and of swelling the expressive content of the first subject.

Motif (b), which sounded in heroic fashion, will be seen to be very much reduced in the recapitulation; the imitations of Ex.112 are renewed between the basses and the first violins, and the shocks imparted to *motif* (b) by imitations in *stretti* are reduced to five bars—not surprising since (b) had borne by itself practically all the burden of the portion following the double bar, that is to say, all that takes the place of the normal development in a Sonata Form movement.

And now, this time, all the fugued passage on (a) forming the opening of the second section has entirely vanished; the *cantabile* subject returns, and the entire third section is reproduced with no alterations save some changes in the disposition of the instrumental parts. Our observations on the subject of this third section are therefore applicable anew here; but we must add that the return of the theme to the tonic and the repetition of the final refrain or *ritornello* give to the whole an air as of apotheosis; as for the section preceding the double bars, the approach of these provides us again with the surprise of a premature and softened ending. For here we find new repeat marks, separating the final *Coda* clearly from all that has gone before.

We now have arrived at the pathetic moment when Mozart sums the whole thing up by way of conclusion. He finds means to present the component themes of the movement in a new light, inverting the first (a), and superposing the others on it. We might with justice have supposed that Mozart, before writing this *Coda*, (which he could have treated as a simple final *stretto*), had drawn from these themes all they were capable of in point of musical force, of vital energy. But the *Coda* shows us that, without combining them in a regular fugue but giving free rein to the contrapuntal force they conceal, they can still reveal unknown resources and, blending with each other, finally blaze out, in a dazzling display of tonal pyrotechnics.

All here is strictly thematic. After having renewed, *forte*, the imitations on *motif* (b) immediately after the double bar, brusquely attacked by the whole orchestra, we have the initial *motif*, completely transformed, and assuming an expression of distant melancholy; despite all our prevision, the handling of these four notes did not seem to hold the promise of such a result! But the possibilities of genius are limitless, and there is something of magic in this power of renewing the colour and expression of a given theme:

*118

then, suddenly, the melodic *motif* (Ex.113) emerges in the violas, likewise transformed by a brusque fugal attack, while the first subject is stated by basses, bassoons and horns. Then the sequel (Ex.112), and another figure, first heard on the oboe immediately after the melodic subject in the third section of the movement (bar 76), join in the combat. Very soon afterwards all the combatant forces find themselves in the struggle, in a page wherein the maximum of intrinsic power of the different themes, the climax of their vital energy, their cohesion, is attained by the master with the most complete success. Now that the great encounter has been joined their *élan* becomes clearer; these elements, immeasurably ennobled by battle, are merged and resolved in a return of the refrain that followed the first subject. Once again (b) re-echoes in unison, and Mozart marks the conclusion with a fanfare, heroic and brief.

. . . . .

Despite the enormous musical weightiness of this symphonic testament of Mozart it can scarcely be affirmed that the 'Jupiter' symphony received the unanimous approval or the almost immediate acclamation of the E flat and G minor symphonies; perhaps the vast plan of the work and especially the complexity of the finale perplexed its first hearers. The fact is that before this masterly *chef-d'œuvre* criticism itself was also dumbfounded. Had not Mozart here pushed his audacities beyond permissible bounds? Again, did he not rely too much on the skill of the performers? A multitude of petty reasons cropped up, as usual in the presence of a still unknown great work. For, with not the slightest risk of self-deception, we can say that nothing so great and important had arisen before that which dawned on 10th August 1788; neither in the orchestra nor in any chamber music centre had a comparable work been heard. And now behold Mozart with his bold felicity, for what reason we know not, raising up this brilliant edifice and crowning it with a vast instrumental 'chorus' which saw the older music, suddenly revived, united with the new to salute the future! With a sovereign grace, eloquence and force, the master in his thirty-second year gathers up all the elements his most glorious predecessors have used and reveals to us all that music has achieved up to his time, and what it will do nearly a hundred years later. That such a work should have proved too difficult for some hearers need not surprise us . . . If, as we have said, this brilliant edifice has apparently been in shadow, fringed by the dark clouds of the romantic period, today it appears even more radiant, elegant and proud than in the past. It is raised up in all its C major brightness to the open sky.

In our delving into past criticisms we have already remarked on a notice almost certainly concerned with the 'Jupiter' (see page 97). In the following article from the pen of the composer Michel Bourges, who replaced Hector Berlioz on *La Gazette Musicale*, dated 5th March 1843, the lack of understanding and appreciation of the most remarkable work of the preceding generation is borne upon us in the clearest fashion:

'Symphony in C, by Mozart'

'In this, despite its elegance, its charm of detail, and despite the enormous facility of the writer, we find too many out-of-date formulae, too many needless commonplaces, too much aimless and purposeless development, too many laborious technical procedures, especially in the finale. The skill of the performers can doubtless fascinate and create illusions, but it could not prevent the *Adagio* from being diffuse and dragging, nor the last movement from being cold and meaningless, despite its admirable construction—a perfect academic model.' In the following year Stephen Heller, in the same journal, praises the *Andante* and the finale, but regards this finale as being 'insolently fugal' (February 1844).

The means of expression chosen by Mozart is, in fact, no longer understood. From the moment fugue appears on the scene, it is argued, he sheds his soul. And we are both surprised and pleased to have been able to quote a French critic of some thirty years earlier, much nearer to grasping the fundamental musical meaning of this masterpiece.

It is true that Wagner, about 1830 or 1831, took it as a direct model in composing his one and only symphony. 'After several other works I set to work on a symphony; to my prototype Beethoven was added Mozart, especially his great C major symphony.'[89] But we shall have occasion to return again to the composer of *Tristan* who, taking the 'Jupiter' symphony as a pattern

[89] Wagner, *Autobiographical sketches.*

153

when he ventured into the realm of the symphony at the outset of his career, remained faithful to Mozart's great work, and discussed it several times in his advice to conductors (1869).

To return to Oulibicheff, who concludes his study[90] of Mozart's symphonies with something resembling a musical ode, —an expression he himself uses to qualify the C major symphony:

'One might say that the symphony in C was commanded and written to celebrate some mighty event in the world's history, a victory of the human mind for ever memorable and blessed, accomplished in humanity's own interests. The resounding splendour of the orchestra bursting forth in all its power at the ninth bar establishes beyond all doubt the attitude of triumphant rejoicing as the fundamental character of the work; but the theme preceding this victorious outburst is a double one; it is composed of a species of fanfare, succeeded by a little interrogatory phrase, in slurred notes. The latter is the main *motif*, the fecund theme that by its developments imprints a unique stamp of spirituality to the great jubilation of the *Allegro*, appealing to the mind as a continued aspiration towards some intellectual summit the lyric poet burns to attain, but can only achieve towards the very end of the ode. Nothing is more magnificent than the amplifications, transformations and analyses of these two thematic fragments. The one sounds and resounds like some forest cascade, repeated in several keys by the mountain echoes; the other figure, ever pursuing under diverse forms the goal to which it aspires, now plunges into the bass or floats above in the melody, now concentrated in a vigorous unison, mounting, mounting, it forces a passage between pedal points in the extreme parts of the score, reinforced by a prolonged play of trumpets. An inexpressible, sublime effect! The middle section, one of the finest examples of "working-out" extant, is constructed for the most part on an accessory theme. This is the delicious, unforgettable violin melody, to a *pizzicato* accompaniment, which, transposed from the dominant (the key in which it is first heard) to E flat major, is now treated as a subject

[90] Oulibicheff, *Nouvelle Biographie de Mozart*, vol. iii, p. 260.

and forms the contrapuntal material. Towards the end this phrase returns in the tonic as a melody with an increase of charm and delight.'

Using no technicalities whatever and with not one quotation Oulibicheff succeeds in giving us a clear idea of the subjects that make up this first movement and of the treatment they undergo. It is an analysis as poetic as it is exact. Moreover, merely in the chapter devoted to the symphonies, many passages of the Russian critic conjure up so vivid an image that it is impressed immediately on the mind, a picture that it is a great pity one cannot reproduce, since it so astonishingly translates and illustrates the musical idea. We cannot resist quoting the following passage dealing with the *Andante*:

'*Andante*, F major, 3/4. Whether a slow movement follows a movement of energetic passion and suffering, or an outburst of jubilation such as the first *Allegro* of this symphony, it always marks that point of repose, of quietude and relaxation, of cessation, that follows great disturbances of the soul. Here the interruption of the ode, the *Andante*, is a picture of calm felicity, of the most profound enchantment. The theme, ravishing in expression, and as singable as any vocal melody,[91] occupies less space than Mozart usually accords to the first subject and its derivatives in the construction of a movement; and this fact attaches importance to the profusion of accessory ideas, to the number and singular euphony of the rival *motifs*. This quantity of beautiful musical detail, interspersed by long passages in demi-semiquavers and in sextolets, these phrases multiplied by themselves in their repetitions and imitations, shed a sort of twilight over the movement, in which the ear loses itself with delight, as the eye of a spectator in a thicket pierced by the rays of the setting sun, illuminating and inflaming it, peopling it with a thousand fantastic visions. Nevertheless, thick, heavy clouds from time to time blot out the blue sky; the sharp thorn of grief is felt in the soul; painful syncopations trouble the harmony; the minor mode breaks out and dominates the scene, in a sequence of phrases quivering with fear; but this smoke without

[91] It is the finest example of the *Cantabile* in instrumental style.

fire, these unsubstantial scarecrows, sport of capricious breeze, appear at random and disappear likewise. The sun triumphs over all these feeble portents of bad weather, his burning disc reappears with the theme, the heart expands under the rays of an ineffable beatitude.'

We cannot think of reproducing here the description of the finale of the 'Jupiter' given by the author. It must suffice to mention that for Oulibicheff 'the fugue in C is Mozart's master-piece in the symphonic *genre*, and the highest expression of the *genre* itself: *der höchste Standpunkt*, a German critic has said': comparing the C major symphony to a musical ode which had achieved the summits, it is logical, concludes the author, 'that since the musical ode could go no farther, Mozart composed no more symphonies.'

With regard to the minuet of this symphony there is an almost universal error in interpretation. As far back as 1843 Oulibicheff remarked that 'the composer's lyrical emotion is rekindled to burst out with a furious gaiety in the minuet *Allegretto*, 3/4, which is usually taken *Allegro*'[92]. Some twenty-five years later Richard Wagner said the same thing even more insistently:

' . . . Nevertheless, I believe Haydn's minuets are generally taken too quickly; undoubtedly the minuets of Mozart's sym-phonies are; this will be felt very distinctly if, for instance, the minuet in Mozart's symphony in G minor, and still more that of his symphony in C major, be played a little slower than at the customary pace. It will be found that the latter minuet which is usually hurried and treated almost as a *Presto*, will now show a quite different character combining grace with impres-sive strength; in contrast with which, the trio, with its delicately sustained rhythm is reduced, as usually given, to an empty hurry-scurry.' [93]

The insistence with which the composer of *Tristan* dis-cusses the great symphonies of Mozart and the authentic way of interpreting them proves that they alone held in his mind a

[92] Oulibicheff, *op. cit.*, iii, p. 263.

[93] Wagner, *The Art of Conducting*, tr. Dannreuther, p. 26.

place worthy of being next to Beethoven's. And that is so true
that he notes an analogy between the two themes of the finale of
the 'Jupiter' and the opening theme of Beethoven's 'Eroica'.[94]
He remarks that these themes scarcely differ from each other,
and he presents them in the following order;

*119

*120

*121

At the same time he is led to make another comparison, to
which we have previously alluded, between the finale of
Mozart's E flat symphony and that of Beethoven's A major;
and for these movements 'wherein the figuration overwhelms
the melody' the opinion of Wagner is that they 'cannot be taken
with too much decision or swiftness.'[95]

. . . . .

Can it be said that the foregoing is the last step in what we
have called 'Mozart's symphonic evolution'? At first sight one
would be tempted to believe so. But we shall have to show that
the master pursued his efforts further, and that his conception
of orchestral writing during the last few months of his existence
was no longer quite that which his three great symphonies offer
us. The finale of the 'Jupiter' did perhaps serve as a step towards the instrumental preface to that really extraordinary and,
if one may say so, unclassifiable work, the *Magic Flute*. That
Mozart has here written an overture and scenes which are
properly symphonic masterpieces, in the most modern sense of

[94] Wagner, *The Art of Conducting*.
[95] *Ibid.*

the word, we need hardly trouble to prove—if only by the treatment of the woodwind in particular, and more generally by the way the strings are united with the wind. But that did not hinder Mozart, hard pressed by circumstances, from writing at about the same time a symphonic page for the opening of his drama *La Clemenza di Tito* which still suggests pretty closely the first *Allegro* of the 'Jupiter'.[96] So his great and last symphony remained firmly fixed in his memory despite later changes of style.

It is not possible to pass over in silence a long and heavy task imposed on Mozart by his learned friend Baron van Swieten, and which was certainly not without a profound influence on the destiny of his art. Towards the autumn of 1788—one of the most astonishing years for rich productiveness—this wealthy patron took it into his head that, though the oratorios of Handel were things of great beauty, the arias offered a certain monotony to the listener. If these arias were re-orchestrated, enhanced by parts for the wind, their musical beauty would be not only more striking but more accessible to the audiences of 1789-1790 —that is to say, for them more 'modern'. And who better fitted than Mozart to accomplish this task? And pressed by domestic worries and urged on by his natural good nature, Mozart set to work; as early as November 1788 the revision of *Acis and Galatea* was finished. The undertaking occupied nearly two years. In March 1789 it was one of the most famous masterpieces of the older master, the *Messiah*, then, in July 1790, the *Ode to Saint Cecilia* and *Alexander's Feast*.

We shall leave on one side the question of the legitimacy of this revision. It must suffice to say that, in 1788-1790, no one saw anything incongruous in these retouches, and that van Swieten was guided solely by the desire to revive the whole of Handel's work; as for Mozart, judging by the amount of work accomplished by him it seems that he quickly acquired a taste for the work, which was after all a much more worthy task than was to be reserved for him in the near future. It was in fact

[96] *La Clemenza di Tito*, commissioned for the Coronation of the Emperor Leopold II, was produced in Prague on 6th Sept. 1791.

during these last years of his life that his court duties compelled him to provide the Assembly Halls of Vienna with dance tunes; the overburdening task of supplying wind parts to arias from oratorios originally scored for strings only was certainly one quite different for the mind from compiling sets of dances suitable for Carnival use in these same years. We have seen Mozart already dipping delightedly into the study of Bach and Handel, at the instigation of van Swieten, at the time of his first Viennese symphony or *serenade*, in 1782. We see him now for more than two years in direct contact with Handel's work, we might almost say with the composer himself. This is a fact of undeniable importance which we must now take into consideration, since we have said that Mozart's symphonic activity was not cut short even though he wrote no more symphonies.

I do not know that one can easily visualise what the solution of such a problem would be for Mozart, arrived at the climax of his artistic career. It was a question of adorning with all the newly acquired riches the somewhat bare statue of the giant carved in stone about 1740. And in clothing and ornamenting it the same stone had to be used so that no foreign intervention should be apparent. As the major part of Mozart's work rests on the wind instruments it may perhaps be permissible to suppose that the master's supreme facility and the preference he evinced for these instruments during the last years of his life found in this work a considerable exercise, a food such as perhaps no original creation could have provided. And moreover, this intercourse with the masters of the past was perhaps already active at the time of the composition of the finale to the 'Jupiter' —without taking into account Mozart's own affinities, which had for a long time been drawing him nearer to the great man, himself no stranger to Italy, in whom the German genius incarnate was not unmixed with a quite different alloy.

The fact is that during the accomplishment of his task as arranger, while he is dispensing the treasures of his contrapuntal science (revivified by contact with Handel); while the wind in scintillating variety was re-echoing its brilliance in his ears, and being superposed in vast columns and in complete independence over Handel's string parts; while Mozart was thus trying to enrich the art of the older master with the modern spirit, his own genius was being impregnated, or rather intoxicated, by these ancient sources.

The result, as much in the realm of chamber music as in the orchestral field, was some works wherein counterpoint is woven into the very roots of the work, serving as a canvas for inventions of the richest kind, both extremely bold and solid. Between the truly astounding finale of his last string quartet (June 1790) and the masterly quintet in D (December of the same year), he passed the whole of the month of July in scoring, in 'modern' style, Handel's *Alexander's Feast* and the *Ode to Saint Cecilia.*

How is it possible not to take account of these facts, and not to see that this work was still echoing in his mind when he wrote the overture and the symphonic ensembles of the *Magic Flute?* And when it comes to the final *Requiem* this influence becomes visible to the extent of finding a Handelian theme in one of the most famous ensembles of the work! In this is to be seen the fruit of study and contact with one of the greatest and richest masters of all music, a study that served to provide Mozart with one of the last musical satisfactions of his brief existence and to hand down to us the ineffable beauty of the first orchestral page of the *Requiem.*

· · · · ·

We know only too well, alas, what were the mental neglect and material privations of Mozart's last years. His orchestra, between the great symphonies and the *Magic Flute,* had to be content to re-echo in the Vienna *Redoutensäle,* accompanying dances, masked balls and annual celebrations. There he dedicated to the nobility his series of Minuets, and to the more humble classes his German Dances and his Ländler. One might say that these works, which form real orchestral suites, ending with grand symphonic *Codas,*[97] are almost totally unknown.

[97] See particularly K. 568, 571, 585, 586, 599, 600, 602, 604, 606.

But, both by the miraculous beauty of their melodies and the inexhaustible variety and unexpectedness of their 'symphonic' or picturesque strokes of genius,[98] these often represent for us a continuation, quite forgotten, of Mozart's instrumental or orchestral progress. Many a delicious surprise would arise today from a performance of these dances, written for a very large orchestra, with a refinement and a noble, a beautiful poetry, sometimes also with so much simplicity and humour that one might imagine one can already hear the Viennese rhythms of Schubert. In pursuing his humble task, in fulfilling his official mission, Mozart has again, within the limits of a fixed framework, found the means of creating a beauty of an order infinitely superior to what was due in such a case.

There is too the fact, rightly noted by Herr Abert,[99] that the juxtaposition of courtly and popular dances in a set of 'carnival redoutes' patronised by the Emperor himself provides almost a replica of the ball scene in *Don Giovanni*: we know with what art and skill the master has contrived to alternate the dances appropriate to every order of society in the *salons* of the Spanish grandee, and we have the same again here, at a time when the reigning monarch favoured the bringing together of the different classes; and if the theatre were to present the spectacle of the Viennese dances of 1788 to 1791 we would today as it were be attending the festivities contemporaneous with Mozart's last years. And we must repeat that if these dances were set aside or passed over in silence the great picture we have attempted to depict of the various 'curves' of Mozart's symphonic activity would have lacked some of the final colours he planned to give to his great orchestral vision.

But it is abundantly clear that Mozart, now arrived at the last year of his life, has given us the most convincing testimony,

[98] Some recalling by their titles some political event; war against the Turks, battles; others, fragments of operas then in vogue; others again imitating bizarre instruments, or birds; the trio of one of these is entitled 'The Canary,' and would serve as a basis for an admirable symphonic scherzo. Finally, a *contredanse* entitled *Les Filles malicieuses* seems to indicate a choreographic programme.

[99] *W. A. Mozart*, vol. ii., p. 613 *et seq.*

the most certain proof of the revolution that has been effected in his thought, both in style and orchestration. In regard to the latter the overture to the *Magic Flute* in particular[100] offers us the stupendous example of a work whose form harks back to distant ages, and whose harmony and scoring suggest an entirely modern approach; there is no longer the least subordination of the wind instruments to the strings, but a collaboration wherein each fills a most active and appropriate *rôle*, a kind of sonorous fullness that Mozart had not previously achieved, and which opens the most attractive vistas of the future. Furthermore with the first orchestral page that serves as a prelude to the *Requiem*, the master gives us his last word on his symphonic preoccupations: the return to ancient forms, clothed in harmonies capable of holding the attention of the most modern musicians. The unheard-of audacities practised in the two Fantasias for a mechanical organ, and the finale of his last string quartet, with their predilection for contrapuntal writing, show us what in general Mozart's latest tendencies were; in terms of the symphony they are affirmed in the overture to the *Magic Flute* and the first pages of the *Requiem*; they are of an order so elevated that they cannot but excite an eternal regret for the symphony Mozart would surely have written, had God but allowed him a few more months of life.

[100] Concerning Mozart's orchestration at this time see Oulibicheff, iii, pp. 414 and 437; Abert, ii, pp. 770-775.

CHAPTER FIFTEEN

Joseph Haydn and Mozart's Last Symphonies

W E WERE BOLD ENOUGH to state at the beginning of the preceding chapter that Mozart's last three symphonic monuments dominated not only his entire work, but all the art of the eighteenth century. When we examine the mass of symphonic output in the classical period we make a lengthy halt before the most outstanding personality, before him who is generally considered the true and perhaps unique model for Mozart; before Joseph Haydn, then arrived at his full maturity! There is no doubt that compared with him a number of his compatriots seem rather small figures; but if, when it came to the question of editing the great edition of his works (still, alas! incomplete), many symphonies which had wrongly figured under his name in the early catalogue had to be eliminated, it seems that a number of his compatriots had written what could actually be mistaken for his own—naturally not the more important or characteristic ones. There were in fact in the Viennese school men whose work was far from negligible, offering interesting specimens of the classical or pre-classical symphony, for the most part from the fecund pen of a Wagenseil: for an example, of symphonies contemporaneous with Mozart's life, those of Johann Vanhall, and of Carl Ditters von Dittersdorf, the inspiration of the former often very curiously romantic, the second most picturesque, furnish interesting 'pre-Mozartian' examples; but it is clear that Haydn's genius, his especially friendly relations with Mozart, and the importance of his own symphonic work, prompt research, which moreover does not seem to have been pushed very far.

If in fact it is asked which exactly are the Haydn symphonies that were expressly used by Mozart as models at the time when he reached the apex of his symphonic art, it is with some surprise that one establishes the fact that the most famous of the Esterház master's symphonies date from his London visits—that is to say, from a time when Mozart had already departed this life; and naturally the only ones we are specially concerned with here are those written between 1786 and 1788. About a dozen symphonies are extant, of which the first six were destined for some Paris concerts,[101] and the last, known as the 'Oxford', celebrates Haydn's accession to the doctorate of music in the famous English university in 1788.[102] Among the Parisian symphonies are to be found those named 'The Bear', 'The Hen', and 'The Queen of France', titles which indicate pretty well the need we have always felt for some sort of appellation for pieces of instrumental music.

We might ask whether Mozart knew them, if copies had been able to circulate in Germany before they appeared in Paris; it certainly seems that a symphony in E flat (No.84),[103] from the Paris set, likewise another very remarkable one in C major (No.90), written about 1787, could not have remained a dead letter for the great symphonist Mozart had become just at this precise time; a certain smooth, fluid beauty distinguishes these symphonies profoundly from those Haydn wrote primarily to amuse the public, and allies them to Mozart both in the matter of form and the ideas.

But supposing Mozart to have had the chance of reading or hearing one or the other, how can we find, even in these cases, anything but the framework? Neither their rapid and charming gaiety, nor the rusticity of some of the minuets, nor the greater part of their *Andantes* with variations, with the very frequent alternation of major and minor, nor even the piquant anima-

[101] The concerts of the *Loge Olympique*.

[102] The degree of Doctor of Music was conferred on Haydn at Oxford on 8th July 1791. The 'Oxford' symphony was written for Paris, in 1788. (Tr.)

[103] Numbering according to Breitkopf and Härtel's edition.

tion of the finales—none of these find enduring echoes in the four Mozartian monuments built on the same forms and almost on the same materials. It would be necessary to probe much further back in Joseph Haydn's symphonic career to meet higher ideals and a greater power of thought; despite his fifty years, he sailed entirely in the waters of 'galanterie', and perhaps the cruel news telling him of the premature death of his friend, so dear to him, momentarily gave to his thought something more noble and elevated.[104]

Again, if Mozart, after 1788, had written only the symphony-serenade of 1782 and the 'Linz' symphony (1783), perhaps it would have been possible to speak with more justification of the determining influence of Haydn; but the first movement of that symphony-serenade would certainly have had to be excluded, as it is nothing more than an incisive and audacious *fugato* to which there is nothing equivalent in any Haydn symphony in the period under discussion (1780 to 1790). Haydn's conception, it must be insisted, was at that time far, very far, from Mozart's: and the older master is removed from Mozart, not so much by his orchestral technique, sometimes so elaborate and yet so naturally witty, as by the quality of his ideas and the very depth of his inspiration. Haydn's interior world—since the time of his great 'romantic' crisis noted for the first time by my never to be forgotten master Téodor de Wyzewa,[105] which he had undergone about 1772 or 1773 in the midst of a period of *Sturm und Drang*, —is singularly narrow: we are of course here considering only his symphonic output which, in our opinion, is infinitely surpassed by the last sets of string quartets. In Wyzewa's opinion —since then verified by ourselves many times—Haydn the symphonist between 1780 and 1790, and again in all his later symphonies written in London in his declining years, with one exception—this Haydn is, first and foremost, an 'entertainer'. A marvellous and inexhaustible entertainer, certainly; a man whose richly flavoured and balanced art traces a beautifully poised musical line, linking the soundest learning with the

[104] See particularly No. 99 (written in 1793).
[105] See *Revue des Deux-Mondes*, 15th December 1909.

astonishing rusticity of the minuets, revealing itself sometimes in the most unexpected manner in the course of those furious finales that kindle an exultation *sui generis*, to the verge of distraction. A captivating and healthy distraction, with no unwholesome quality about it, which, far from fatiguing, on the contrary freshens and invigorates like open air exercise. This is the particular contribution of Haydn's work contemporaneous with the great symphonies of Mozart. But how can we explain the enormous 'mental' and expressive superiority of the latter?

To us there is no exaggeration in the claim that it is rather the Haydn of the London symphonies (1791-1795) who at times recalls Mozart,[106] and the overwhelming influence of Haydn's symphonies on those of Mozart's maturity has perhaps been too readily inferred. If we make a direct comparison of two or three of the 'Parisian' symphonies, written by Haydn in 1786, also two or three others composed in 1787 and 1788, with Mozart's symphonies, what do we find? We see works almost identical in form, but differing profoundly in spirit. None of these Haydn symphonies, however ingenious, witty, or solid they may be, betrays for a single moment any hint of the passion, agitation, or uneasiness by which Mozart's great creative mind reveals itself; we find but rarely that fragrance of warm, youthful tenderness that every work written by Mozart exhales; we can find there none of the signs by which we recognize the gifts of that fertile poetic fancy which yielded Mozart so many unexpected strokes of genius. But we strive in vain to describe two absolutely different inner worlds, which have been wrongly considered as having contributed to the formation of each other. We have not, indeed, attempted a pointless and in fact impossible comparison just in order to lead to the ordinary result of exalting one at the expense of the other; we would even say that one of the principal features of the real symphonic style—the elaboration of *motifs*—seems more richly active in Haydn, and much nearer to Beet-

[106] Particularly that magnificent symphony in E flat, written between the two London visits (1793), to which we have just alluded, and which is a sort of supreme homage to Mozart's memory.

hoven's art, than is generally the case with Mozart. But what slow introduction from Haydn's symphonies could we honestly compare with the enormous and significant preludes that open, for instance, Mozart's 'Prague' or E flat symphonies? What amiable *Andante* of the Esterház master dare we bring near the romantic visions of the G minor, of the 'Jupiter'? And what finale of Haydn's can sustain the splendour of the finales of these two symphonies? As a measure of the unbridgeable gulf between the art of the two men, contrast Mozart's last symphonic finale with one of the last and most remarkable of Haydn's, that ending his 'Military' symphony (No.100): although six years later than the 'Jupiter' it is quite evident that this finale has neither the size nor the range of that which concludes Mozart's greatest symphonic work.

How vain is the attempt to establish kinship when such a genius inspires such works! Once arrived at its climax, Mozart's genius, by its very poetic essence and universality, evades all attempt at *rapprochement*. There is no common ground between the close of one age and the beginning of another.

In the symphonic field it would not, however, be difficult to discover in Mozart certain traces of the influence exerted by Haydn; but it would be necessary to go back particularly to the period before he came to settle in Vienna. Moreover, we have already had occasion on a number of preceding pages to note this influence, when we were studying the works written by Mozart during the years 1772-1774. There is incontestably a debt here, contracted by the younger man to the older; but once arrived at full maturity it can be said, in fact, that Mozart draws on himself, and that the treasures of his inner life sufficed him for nourishment. It seems that there was no one among his contemporaries at that time with the power to offer him anything of equal value. Most of these spoke the same language, but without his genius. Even when we examine the symphonies written by Haydn between 1784 and 1788, for example, we certainly cannot see in them the inspiring model of Mozart's great symphonies. The latter, considered solely from the harmonic viewpoint, are portals opening on the future: the imposing opening of the E flat symphony, with its harsh and bold modulations, the mysterious *Andante* of the G minor symphony, the minor passages in the *Andante cantabile* of the 'Jupiter', belong already to the following age, and even presage Wagner; while in comparison the symphonic work of old Haydn, with very rare exceptions, serves as a conclusion to the instrumental art of the eighteenth century. This 'modernism' of Mozart has been appreciated only quite recently; there is decidedly an evolution in the mode of appraising and performing the work of great men: the harmonic boldnesses, so easy to establish, so frequent in the composer of the *Magic Flute*, had been observed only rarely before the time of Fétis, who proposed to correct the introduction of the last of the Haydn quartets. And the same observation might be made with regard to the poetic essence, the universality of human feeling, always stamped with the same formal beauty, which we are beginning to discover in Mozart. It is not so long since critics took it into their heads to compare Mozart to Shakespeare, and that marks a date; perhaps even the special enthusiasm which Mozart prompts in some writers of the younger generation of today proceeds a little from this universal character of his genius—a genius that has no fear of the ridiculous even when it borders on the sublime. No position is more false than that which admits only a certain order of invariable beauty in Mozart's work; one is astonished to see today all the feelings of the human soul in contact with life reflected therein with, in addition, the feeling surpassing all others, that of the mystery of the beyond.

Mozart's last symphonies, then, form a whole which in our opinion dominates all the production of the classical period, including the remarkable work—often unique in its own *genre* —of Joseph Haydn. We have no doubt whatever that Mozart's last symphonies aim at a higher mark than any others which were written in the period of his maturity; not by any means that they speak a different language, or that they were conceived in a revolutionary spirit, tending to repudiate the past and erect something in its place. They spring solely from a brilliant mind, from a man whose inner world surpassed all in richness, in expression and in beauty; Mozart's power of clothing all things from the greatest to the smallest in this beauty remained essentially the privilege of the poet he always was. And he had no need to turn things topsy-turvy, putting the end before the beginning, in order to create novelty; it was only necessary for him to fill the framework with his own thought for everything to be rejuvenated. In the same way the richness and variety of the contrasts with which his work is filled come out more and more clearly today, completely reversing the usual judgements relative to his art conceded by the romantic age:[107] they proceed from his very special aptitude for observing mankind in all the varied manifestations of life, for grasping a foreign tongue, down to the least inflexion, with an alertness and delicacy rare among his compatriots. This is not the least of our surprises in the presence of Mozart; it is evident that throughout almost the whole of his life he had the clearest appreciation of Italian *buffa* art, whose technique was appropriated by him to a degree unexampled and unforeseeable; it was not only the formal beauty of the Italian musical phrase as adopted sentimentally by a Christian Bach, but a leaning towards the most biting and delicate satire, which, indeed, was quite in keeping with his own character. On reflection one realizes that he even surpasses his model by the full extent of his own genius, and, as Herr Abert has so justly remarked, Mozart seems to smile on the personages he creates, but who, one feels, are so very different from him.

Commentators have been specially led to analyse these marvellous gifts in the stage works. We have wished to be sufficiently discerning to attempt to illustrate them from his instrumental works, and particularly here in his great symphonies. The latter seem to us the most absolute witness, the most intimate revelations of his 'ego'; and we feel that a long companionship with such masterpieces has not sufficed to reveal all the treasures of their profound and moving beauty. As with all great creators the secret of this beauty is not fully

[107] See the psychological analysis of Mozart's personality, already noted above: Abert, ii, p. 1-36.

revealed at first sight; however, we cannot help being astonished that it has needed nearly a century and a half for people to discover in Mozart anything other than grace and charming elegance. This miraculous artist, as Téodor de Wyzewa used to style him, in his last symphonies does in fact reveal to us the true world inhabited by his soul at the moment when it is turning towards other regions. The fact is that from 1789 or 1790 the very source of Mozart's inspiration changes; a sort of purification, accompanied often by a feeling of resigned lassitude, gives to his work a beauty removed from all passion, purged of all anxiety, testifying to an almost celestial calm. His last three symphonies seem definitely to set the seal on the most 'romantic' period of all his career, in which the ardent tumult of life is quelled only to allow him time to ascend to even higher regions.

APPENDIX

BIBLIOGRAPHY

INDEX

APPENDIX

A list of the symphonic works of Mozart

(The dates given in this list, which differ in some respects from those in the body of the work, are taken from Einstein's revision of Köchel's Catalogue [1937]. Where his revised numbers differ from those of Köchel's original classification these are given in brackets alongside the original.)

Köchel No.		Scoring	Date and place of composition
16	No. 1	in E flat, 2 vlns, vla, bass, 2 oboes, 2 horns	London 1764 or early 1765
17 (Anh. 223a)	No. 2	in B flat, 2 vlns, vla, bass, 2 oboes, 2 horns	London 1764 or early 1765
18 (Anh. 109i)	No. 3	in E flat, 2 vlns, vla, bass, 2 clts, 2 horns, bassoon	London (copied) 1764
19	No. 4	in D, 2 vlns, vla, bass, 2 oboes, 2 horns	London 1765
22	No. 5	in B flat, 2 vlns, vla, bass, 2 oboes, 2 horns	The Hague, Dec. 1765
43	No. 6	in F, 2 vlns, vla, bass, 2 oboes, 2 horns (oboes replaced by Flutes in the *Andante*)	Vienna-Olmütz Dec. 1767
45	No. 7	in D, 2 vlns, vla, bass, 2 oboes, 2 horns, tpts, kettledrums	Vienna 16th Jan. 1768
48	No. 8	in D, 2 vlns, vla, bass, 2 oboes, 2 horns, tpts, kettledrums	Vienna 13th Dec. 1768
73 (75a)	No. 9	in C, 2 vlns, vla, bass, 2 oboes, 2 horns, tpts, kettledrums	Salzburg, summer 1771
74	No. 10	in G, 2 vlns, vla, bass, 2 oboes, 2 horns	Milan, Dec. 1770

[108] Those symphonies where no date is given were first published in Breitkopf and Härtel's complete edition of Mozart's works.

Köchel No.		Scoring	Date and pla of compositio
75	No. 42	in F, 2 vlns, vla, bass, 2 oboes, 2 horns	Salzburg 1771
76 (42a)	No. 43	in F, 2 vlns, vla, bass, 2 oboes, 2 horns, 2 bassoons	Vienna, autur 1767
81 (73l)	No. 44	in D, 2 vlns, vla, bass, 2 oboes, 2 horns	Rome, 25th April 1770
84 (73q)	No. 11	in D, 2 vlns, vla, bass, 2 oboes, 2 horns	Milan and Bologna, 1770
95 (73n)	No. 45	in D, 2 vlns, vla, bass, 2 oboes, 2 horns, 2 tpts	Rome, 25th April 1770
96 (111b)	No. 46	in C, 2 vlns, vla, bass, 2 oboes, 2 horns, 2 tpts, kettledrums	Milan, Oct.- Nov. 1771
97 (73m)	No. 47	in D, 2 vlns, vla, bass, 2 oboes, 2 horns, 2 tpts, kettledrums	Rome, April 1770
98 (Anh. 223b)	No. 48	in F, 2 vlns, vla, bass, 2 oboes, 2 horns	Milan?, 1771
99 (63a)		Cassation in B flat, 2 vlns, vla, bass, 2 oboes, 2 horns	Salzburg, sum mer 1769
100 (62a)		Serenade in D, 2 vlns, vla, bass, 2 horns, 1 tpt, 2 oboes	Salzburg, sum mer 1769
110 (75b)	No. 12	in G, 2 vlns, vla, bass, 2 oboes, 2 horns (2 flutes and 2 bassoons in the *Andante*)	Salzburg, July 1771
112	No. 14	in F, 2 vlns, vla, bass, 2 oboes, 2 horns	Milan, 2nd N 1771
114	No. 14	in A, 2 vlns, vla, bass, 2 flutes, 2 horns	Salzburg, 30t Dec. 1771

First edition	Number of movements	Reference page
	4. Allegro – Menuetto – Andantino–Allegro (Rondeau)	30
	4. Allegro maestoso – Andante –Menuetto – Allegro	18
	3. Allegro – Andante – Allegro molto	28
	3. Allegro – Andante – Allegro	28
	4. Allegro – Andante – Menuetto – Allegro	27-8
	4. Allegro – Andante – Menuetto – Allegro molto	38-40
	4. Allegro – Andante – Menuetto – Presto	27-8
	4. Allegro – Andante – Menuetto – Presto	30
	7. Marcia – Allegro molto – Andante – Menuetto – Andante - Menuetto - Allegro	19
	8. Allegro – Andante – Menuetto – Allegro – Menuetto – Andante – Menuetto – Allegro	19
	4. Allegro – Andante – Menuetto – Allegro	30
	4. Allegro – Andante – Menuetto – Molto Allegro (Rondeau)	30-31
	4. Allegro moderato – Andante – Menuetto – Molto Allegro	33

Köchel No.		Scoring	Date and Place of Composition
124	No. 15	in G, 2 vlns, vla, bass, 2 oboes, 2 horns	Salzburg, 2nd Feb. 1772
128	No. 16	in C, 2 vlns, vla, bass, 2 oboes, 2 horns	Salzburg, May 1772
129	No. 17	in G, 2 vlns, vla, bass, 2 oboes, 2 horns	Salzburg, May 1772
130	No. 18	in F, 2 vlns, vla, bass, 2 flutes, 2 horns (in F), 2 horns (in C)	Salzburg, May 1772
132	No. 19	in E flat, 2 vlns, vla, bass, 2 oboes, 4 horns (E flat)	Salzburg, July 1772
133	No. 20	in D, 2 vlns, vla, bass, 2 oboes, 2 horns, tpts (flute obbligato in the *Andante*)	Salzburg, July 1772
134	No. 21	in A, 2 vlns, vla, bass, 2 flutes, 2 horns	Salzburg, Aug. 1772
162	No. 22	in C, 2 vlns, vla, bass, 2 oboes, 2 horns, 2 tpts	Salzburg, autumn 1773
181 (162b)	No. 23	in D, 2 vlns, vla, bass, 2 oboes, 2 horns, 2 tpts	Salzburg, May 1773
182 (166c)	No. 24	in B flat, 2 vlns, vla, bass, 2 oboes, 2 horns	Salzburg, May or June 1773
183	No. 25	in G minor, 2 vlns, vla, bass, 2 horns (in G), 2 horns (in B flat), 2 bassoons	Salzburg, end of 1773
184 (166a)	No. 26	in E flat, 2 vlns, vla, bass, 2 oboes, 2 bassoons, 2 horns, 2 tpts	Salzburg, autumn 1773

Köchel No.		Scoring	Date and place of composition
199 (162a)	No. 27	in G, 2 vlns, vla, bass, 2 flutes, 2 horns	Salzburg, April 1773
200 (173e)	No. 28	in C, 2 vlns, vla, bass, 2 oboes, 2 horns, 1 bassoon, 2 tpts	Salzburg, Nov 1773
201 (186a)	No. 29	in A, 2 vlns, vla, bass, 2 oboes, 2 horns	Salzburg, early 1774
202 (186b)	No. 30	in D, 2 vlns, vla, bass, 2 oboes, 2 horns, 2 tpts	Salzburg, 5th May 1774
239		*Serenata Notturna* in D, string quartet and string orchestra, kettledrums	Salzburg, Jan. 1776
250 (248b)		Serenade in D, 2 vlns, vla, bass, 2 oboes, 2 bassoons, 2 horns, 2 tpts	Salzburg, July 1776
286 (269a)		*Notturno*, in D, for 4 orchestras, each of 2 vlns, vla, bass, 2 horns	Salzburg, Dec. 1776 to Jan. 1777
297 (300a)	No. 31	in D, 2 vlns, vla, bass, 2 flutes, 2 oboes, 2 clts, 2 bassoons, 2 horns, 2 tpts, kettledrums	Paris, 12th June 1778
318	No. 32	in G, 2 vlns, vla, bass, 2 flutes, 2 oboes, 2 bassoons, 4 horns, 2 tpts	Salzburg, 26th April 1779
319	No. 33	in B flat, 2 vlns, vla, bass, 2 oboes, 2 bassoons, 2 horns	Salzburg, 9th July 1779
320		Serenade in D, 2 vlns, vla, bass, 2 flutes, 2 oboes, 2 bassoons, 2 horns, 2 tpts., kettledrums (posthorn in 2nd Menuetto)	Salzburg, 3rd Aug. 1779

First edition	Number of movements	Reference page
Günther and Böhme (Hamburg). Op. 64. No. III. 1799	3. Allegro – Andantino grazioso – Presto	46-7
	4. Allegro spiritoso - Andante - Menuetto – Presto	47-50
	4. Allegro moderato – Andante – Menuetto – Allegro con spirito	47-50
Günther and Böhme (Hamburg). Op. 64. No. IV. 1799	4. Molto Allegro – Andantino con moto – Menuetto – Presto	47-50
	3. Marcia. Maestoso – Menuetto – Rondeau. Allegretto	57
	10. Allegro maestoso – Allegro molto – Andante – Menuetto – Rondo – Menuetto galante - Andante – Menuetto – Adagio – Allegro assai	55-6
	3. Andante – Allegretto grazioso – Menuetto	57-8
Sieber (Paris) 1789	3. Allegro assai – Andantino – Allegro	63-5, 67
Imbault (Paris) before 1792	2. Allegro spiritoso – Andante	71-2, 74, 76
Artaria (Vienna) 1785	4. Allegro assai – Andante moderato – Menuetto – Finale. Allegro assai	72-3
André (Offenbach). Op. 22. 1792	7. Adagio. Maestoso – Allegro con spirito – Menuetto – Concertante. Andante grazioso – Andantino – Menuetto – Finale	73-4

Köchel No.		Scoring	Date and place of composition
338	No. 34	in C, 2 vlns, vla, bass, 2 oboes, 2 bassoons, 2 horns, tpts, kettledrums	Salzburg, 29th Aug. 1780
364 (320d)		Concertante for violin and viola, in E flat, 2 vlns, vla, bass, 2 oboes, 2 horns	Salzburg, summer 1779
385	No. 35	in D, 2 vlns, vla, bass, 2 oboes, 2 horns, 2 bassoons, tpts., kettledrums	Vienna, July-Aug 1782
425	No. 36	in C, 2 vlns, vla, bass, 2 oboes, 2 horns, 2 bassoons, tpts, kettledrums	Linz, 3rd Nov. 1783
444 (425a)	No. 37	in G, 2 vlns, vla, bass, 2 oboes, 2 horns (flute extra in *Andante*)	*Adagio* added, Linz, Nov. 1783
477 (479a)		C minor, *Maurerische Trauermusik*, 2 vlns, vla, bass, 2 oboes, 1 clt, 2 horns, 3 basset horns, 1 double bassoon	Vienna, 10th Nov. 1785
504	No. 38	in D, 2 vlns, vla, bass, 2 flutes, 2 oboes, 2 bassoons, 2 horns, tpts, kettledrums	Vienna, 6th Dec. 1786
522		in F, 2 vlns, vla, bass, 2 horns	Vienna, 14th June 1787
543	No. 39	in E flat, 2 vlns, vla, bass, 1 flute, 2 clts, 2 bassoons, 2 horns, 2 tpts, kettledrums	Vienna, 26th June 1788
550	No. 40	in G minor, 2 vlns, vla, bass, 1 flute, 2 bassoons, 2 horns	Vienna, 25th July 1788
551	No. 41	in C, 2 vlns, vla, bass, 1 flute, 2 oboes, 2 bassoons, 2 horns, 2 tpts., kettledrums	Vienna, 10th Aug. 1788

. . . . .

First edition	Number of movements	Reference page
André (Offenbach). Op.57. 1797	3. Allegro vivace – Andante di molto – Finale. Allegro vivace	75-7
André (Offenbach). Op.104. 1801	3. Allegro maestoso - Andante- Presto	74-5
Artaria (Vienna) 1785	4. Allegro con spirito – Andante – Menuetto – Finale. Presto	80-2, 165
André (Offenbach). Op.34. 1793	4. Adagio. Allegro spiritoso – Poco Adagio – Menuetto – Presto	82-4, 165
	3. Adagio. [Allegro con spirito– Andante sostenuto – Allegro molto]	84-5
André (Offenbach). Op.114. About 1805	1. Adagio	85-6
André (Offenbach. Op.84. 1800	3. Adagio. Allegro – Andante – Finale. Presto	87-90, 167
André (Offenbach. Op.93. About 1801	4. Allegro – Menuetto. Maestoso – Adagio cantabile – Presto	91-3
André (Offenbach). Op.58. 1797	4. Adagio. Allegro – Andante con moto – Menuetto. Allegretto – Finale. Allegro	76, 94, 99—113, 123, 133, 152, 157, 167-8, 170
André (Offenbach). Op.45. 1794	4. Molto Allegro – Andante – Menuetto. Allegretto – Allegro assai	95-9, 109-10, 114-34, 143, 152, 167-8, 170
André (Offenbach. (Op.38. 1793	4. Allegro vivace – Andante cantabile – Menuetto. Allegretto – Molto Allegro	81, 95, 97, 99, 110, 133, 134-159, 167-8, 170

. . . . .

Köchel No.	Scoring	Date and place of composition
Auh. 8 (311a)	Overture in B flat, 2 vlns, vla, bass, 2 flutes, 2 oboes, 2 clts, 2 bassoons, 2 horns, 2 tpts, kettledrums	Paris, Aug.-Sept. 1778
Anh.9 (297b)	in E flat, 2 vlns, vla, bass, 2 oboes, 2 horns	Paris, 5-20th April, 1778
Auh. 100 (383g)	in E flat, 2 vlns, vla, bass, flute, 2 oboes, 2 horns, bassoon	Vienna Spring 1787
Anh.214 (45b)	in B flat, 2 vlns, vla, bass, 2 oboes, 2 horns	Vienna, early 1768
Anh. 215 (66c)	lost	Salzburg, end of 1769
Anh. 216 (74g)	in B flat, 2 vlns, vla, bass, 2 oboes, 2 horns	Salzburg,1771
Anh. 217 (66d)	lost	Salzburg, end of 1769
Anh. 218 (66e)	lost	Salzburg, end of 1769
Anh. 221 (45a)	in G, 2 vlns, vla, bass, 2 oboes, 2 horns	Vienna, early 1768

. . . . .

First edition	No. of movements	Reference page
L'Imprimerie du Conservatoire (Paris) about 1805	1. Andante & Allegro conspirito spirituoso	65-9
Unpublished	3. Allegro – Adagio – Andantino con variazione	61
Unpublished	2. Andante - Allegro	109
Unpublished	4. Allegro – Andante – Menuetto – Allegro	30
	—	30
Breitkopf and Härtel (Leipzig).Apr.1910	4. Allegro – Andante – Menuetto – Allegro molto	30-1
Unpublished	—	30
Unpublished	—	30
Unpublished	3. Allegro maestoso – Andante – Presto	21-3

. . . . .

BIBLIOGRAPHY

Abert (Hermann).—*W. A. Mozart* (5th edition of Otto Jahn's *Mozart*), Leipzig, Breitkopf & Härtel (1921), 2 vols. See, on the symphonies, vol. ii, p. 398–401; 567-603.

Ambros (A.W.).—*Grenzen der Poesie und der Musik* (1856). On the symphony in E flat, p. 123.

Apel (A.).—Poem on the E flat symphony (called Swan Song). See *Allgemeine Musikalische-Zeitung*, viii, p. 453-7 and 465-70.

Bacher (Otto).—*Ein Mozartfund. Zeitschr. f. Musikwiss.*, January 1926, p. 226 et seq.

Brenet (Michel).—*Histoire de la Symphonie à orchestre jusqu'à Beethoven* (1882).

Botstiber (H.).—*Geschichte der Ouvertüre*, Leipzig, 1913.

Cocatrix.—*Correspondance des Amateurs Musiciens* (1802-5).

Curzon (H. de).—*Lettres de Mozart* (translated into French) 1888 and 1898, 2 vols.

Deldevez (M. E.).—*Curiosités musicales* (1873).

Elwart (A. A. E.).—*Histoire de la Société des Concerts du Conservatoire* (1860).

Fétis (F.J.).—Biographie universelle des Musiciens (1837-44).

Framery et Ginguené.—*Encyclopédie méthodique*, see Momigny.

Gail (J.).—*Réflexions sur le goût musical en France*.

Hoffmann (E. T. A.).—*Fantasiestücke*, i, 4.

Jahn (Otto).—*W. A. Mozart*, 4 editions: 1856-59; 1867; 1889-91; 1905-07. Leipzig, Breitkopf & Härtel.

Kretschmar (A. F. H.).—*Führer durch den Konzertsaal*. Vol. I & II, Leipzig, 1913. See on the Mozart symphonies, II, pp. 168-189.

Köchel (Ludwig, Ritter von).—*Chronologisch-thematisches Verzeichnis*, 1st edition, 1862; 2nd edition (revised by Paul, Graf von Waldersee, 1905).

La Laurencie (Lionel de).—*Le Goût musical en France*, see p. 235.

Mendelssohn (Felix).—Letters, 1833-37.

Momigny (Jérôme Joseph de).—*Encyclopédie méthodique* (2nd vol.), 1818, see page 412 (analysis of the G minor symphony).

Naegeli (H. G.).—*Vorlesungen über Musik* (1826).

Nef (Ch.).—*Geschichte der Sinfonie und Suite* (1921), see 163-167.

Nissen (G. N. von).—*Biographie W. A. Mozart's*, 1828.

Oulibicheff (Alexandre).—*Nouvelle biographie de Mozart*, Moscow, 1843, 3rd vol., pp. 233-271.

Schultz (Detlef).—*Mozart's Jugend-Sinfonien*, Leipzig, 1900.

Schumann (Robert).—*Ges. Schriften*, IV, p. 62 (on a passage in the G minor symphony).

Wagner (Richard).—*Oeuvre d'Art de l'Avenir*, p. 85—*Sur une école allemande de musique (Tome IX)—L'art de diriger l'Orchestre—Une Soirée heureuse—Esquisse autobiographique* (Translated into French by M. J. G. Prod'homme. English translation, in 8 vols.: of the *Gesammelte Schriften*, by W. Ashton Ellis, Richard Wagner's Prose works.)

Wilder (Victor).—*Mozart, l'homme et l'artiste*, 1881.

Wyzewa (Téodor de) et Saint-Foix (Georges de).—*W. A. Mozart, sa vie et son oeuvre, de l'enfance à la pleine maturité*, 2 vols., Paris, Perrin, 1912.

. . . . .

PERIODICALS

Mozart-Jahrbuch, 1st year (1923).—Art. by Wilhelm Fischer, pp. 35-69.

Allgemeine Musikalische-Zeitung, 1798 et seq.

Journal de Paris, 1777-1779.

Mercure de France, 1777-1779.

La Décade Philosophique, An 11—septembre, 1807.

Tablettes de Polymnie, 1810-1811.

Revue Musicale (1828).

La Gazette Musicale (1836-1844).

Musikführer:
   No. 8. Aug. Gluck.—*W. A. Mozart's G moll Symphonie* (1788).
   No. 54. A. Pochammer.—*W. A. Mozart's Symphonie in C dur*.
   No. 69. C. Witting.—*W. A. Mozart's Symphonie in Es dur*.

INDEX

785.11
Sa2

Date Due

MAY 15 '81			
MAR 14 '84			
APR 11 '84			
MAY 2 '84			